Never Complete.
Becoming Who We Were Meant To Be

David Schaub

Copyright © 2017 David Schaub

All rights reserved.

ISBN-13: 978-1981715855

ISBN-10: 198171585

I dedicate this book to my Valley Creek Church Family in Buffalo NY. Without your love and encouragement none of this would have been possible. So much of what is in this book has been absorbed from all of you. I am forever grateful for your support and showing me firsthand how to follow the Jesus.

TABLE OF CONTENTS

INTRODUCTION 5

CHAPTER 1: EVERYONE HAS A STORY TO TELL AND IT'S WORTH BEING HEARD. 11

CHAPTER 2: NEXT STEP LEADERS (TAKING NEXT STEPS SO OTHERS CAN TAKE THEIRS) 29

CHAPTER 3: GRATITUDE- A NEXT STEP WE ALL SHOULD TAKE 41

CHAPTER 4: MENTORSHIP, ENVIRONMENTS, FISH BOWLS AND GUARD RAILS. OH MY 51

CHAPTER 5: HEALTHY RELATIONSHIPS 69

CHAPTER 6: IS BEING BUSY REALLY WORTH IT? 87

CHAPTER 7: THERE IS ALWAYS A NEXT STEP TO TAKE 101

Introduction

"Same Shit, Different Day"

Have you ever heard someone say this in response when you asked, "How's it going?" Think about it. When we see our family members or friends at a get-together, we often ask, "What's going on? Anything new?" What's the usual response? I usually get "nothing" or "same shit, different day." Or something along those lines. How about you? Very rarely do I get an answer with enthusiasm. Am I the only one who thinks that life is a hell of a lot more than "same shit, different day"? Am I the only one who feels that we are made for so much more? That life isn't about going through the same old mundane routine and complaining about how so and so didn't do what they were supposed to do? Can't we have a more meaningful conversation besides what store has the biggest sale around this week? Or what the latest gossip is? Life is so much more than this. I've realized bored people talk about other people. It makes them feel better. Average people talk about events. People who are excited about life talk about the next steps they will take in their lives to become who they are meant to be. Which one are you?

I know that's a strong statement to start off with. That might even come across as judgmental, but I want to call it like it is to start this book. I feel that many of us, including me, can miss the boat on what life is all about. In this book, I want to talk about things that people don't talk about. I want to talk about things that people ignore or just keep down inside them. I want to talk about things we are afraid to let out or feel aren't important enough to bring up. Or maybe if we talked about them, we would be judged or viewed as different. I don't want this to be another book that just motivates someone for a weekend and has no lasting effect. I want this to get to the core of people and make them think differently in a positive way. I want this to draw things out of people that they knew they had in them all along, but they were just too scared to admit or discuss. I feel like I was created to write this and exploit it.

I was always afraid of being different. I wanted to be noticed, but I was afraid of being so different that people might push me away. I have so many thoughts and memories in my head that I just wanted to write these down before I forgot them all. We all have a story to share. We all have something to bring to the world through our unique gifts. I feel like mine was the gift of *influence*, and I would be just plain selfish if I didn't use the gift that God gave me. Or maybe I'm scared that I will come to the end one day and realize I never used it to its full potential. Fear either paralyzes or it propels, and a friend of mine once told me that fear isn't a good way to make decisions. I say my next couple sentences because I need to say it even though I don't believe it all the time. I am here to influence. I am here to share my story, and I am loved. I have the power to change the world one person at a time. We all do. I was meant to write this book.

I am scared to think what people might think of this book, but I am willing to take the risk. We all have risks to take and I'm here to take one so others might be inspired to take their necessary risks in life, to jump when they don't know what will happen next. Life is full of optical illusions that appear as dead-end roads, but in reality, most of these dead-end roads are just choices we must make. In this book, I will share stories that I haven't told everyone and some, no one.

I'm here to say that life does not suck. There is freedom to be had. There is peace in the uncertainty. Life doesn't have to be dragged on just because others are moving forward. We can quiet the storms. We can stop for a minute and actually think about what we are doing with our lives and make the choices that need to be made.

We were meant for greatness and to live fulfilling lives, to break chains that need to be broken, and to love others when it's not fair. We were meant to be vulnerable. The world needs it. Fear will no longer be the reason why I make decisions and why I won't be vulnerable. Or at least I'm going to try it. I won't let fear slow me down when the world tells me I can't succeed because it'll be a waste of time. There will be days and moments I fail in this, but it was never about being perfect. Could it be there is a sort of freedom in saying I don't have it all together?

If I'm being honest with you, it has taken me 6 years to write this book. I've rewritten it two times. I told myself while writing this book that there are better books out there. They can say it better than I; however, just like you, my story is worth being told. And so is yours. That is what drove me to finish this book. Our stories should be shared, and we all have unique purpose and destiny to our lives. We are all at different points in our lives, and we all have a next step to take. This is mine. I just keep learning so much and am afraid I'm going to miss something if I release this book, but I'm not going to let that fear stop me anymore because I'm never going to stop learning. We never graduate from the school of taking next steps. We are never complete. Whether we are 18, 48, or 88, we all have a next step to take. We all have a new destiny to fulfill in order to become who we were created to be. If you're not dead, God is still using you.

Also, I have learned many of the insights in this book from others over the years. I have learned other ideas in this book from personal experience. But also, I have heard a lot of it from previous sermons, books I've read, or mentors in my life. I am a sponge when it comes to absorbing information and anything that will help me in life. I don't think I've been what the world would call successful because I learned anything different or had the "Secret sauce." I just implement ideas I love right away and take one next step at a time.

I'm going to ask rhetorical questions in this book and say things that might sound like I am questioning my convictions. Believe me, I am not. I want permission from you to dive deeper even though I'm not physically with you. I want you to decide whether to move forward or not with your next step. In the end, we all make our own decisions for our lives. Life is about choices. I don't want to preach or come across as a know-it-all. I just want to share my story and what I've learned.

I don't want this book to just entertain you or make you feel good about yourself. That's why we have YouTube Videos. I want this book to inspire you to take your next step, and I want that next step to inspire you to take more. We can't always start in big leaps, and in fact, most stories don't start that way. Mine didn't. I urge you to not read this book in one sitting. Please stop and answer the questions after each chapter. Physically write your answers in this book. Mark it up and highlight. I want you to digest everything this book has to offer. I just want people to focus on their next step every day despite popularity, apathy of others, or how difficult it might be at times. Despite all that, we have a choice every day to take a next step. What's a next step exactly? I'm glad you asked…

A next step is moving forward with anything that brings you into greater freedom and purpose.

I'm excited to share my story and encourage you to keep taking next steps as you read this book. Not all at once, but one step at a time. I also encourage you to read this and stop to ask yourself the questions at the end of every chapter. Physically write the answers in this book and plan your next step. It will be very obvious to you what next step you will need to take. We all have one. Mine was finally finishing this book. I am taking my next step so you, the reader, can take yours.

Chapter 1: Everyone Has a Story to Tell and It's Worth Hearing.

My Story

My poison was performance. It still can be. We all have a poison in our lives that we struggle with. Some can be looking for love in the wrong places. Others can be putting their identity in money. Mine was if I do enough, I will be enough. *If I can do (fill in the blank), I will be worth loving or being accepted.* It wasn't always performance, however. It started with significance. In fact, if you grew up with me, I bet you wouldn't have guessed my downfall was performance. I wasn't a straight A student. I was never the top athlete on the sports team. I didn't have a girlfriend in high school. I wasn't invited to the parties in high school. Not once. I wasn't trying to be the best. I just wanted to be a part of something. I wanted to matter and be accepted. I was the oldest of 5 siblings, and I have a twin brother. We rarely went on vacations as a kid, but my mom did the best she could. It wasn't until after high school that I came out of my shell. That's when I really started hanging out with some new friends, some that I still hang out with today. That's also when I realized something: If I made people laugh and if I said some outlandish things, some people wanted to be around me more. I started to receive invitations to events and parties, and it felt good to be liked and wanted. That's when the cycle of performance started for me. *If I do (fill in the blank) then I could become significant, accepted, wanted or loved.* It wasn't until later that I realized I had the whole thing backwards. Sometimes I felt like a clown who couldn't take off his makeup.

I was arrested four times before I Was 21 years old. I wasn't a bad kid though, and it wasn't as bad as it sounds. I was arrested for setting off fireworks in people's homes, urinating in public while intoxicated on a busy street, and running over people's mailboxes. Remember the whole *if I do boisterous things I would be enough*? When I was 20 years old, I was arrested for beating up a guy at a house party. We both thought we were tough guys, and unfortunately, the other guy ended up in the hospital. That guy also had a Supreme Court judge for an uncle. My lawyer told me that I hit the wrong dude, and I was hit with a felony conviction at the age of 21 on top of being kicked out of college with a .86 GPA. Let's just say, I wasn't on the right track.

I remember when I was first arrested for the fight. I remember how resentful I was towards my family and my father. My father wasn't around most of my childhood. My parents were divorced when I was four. My dad went to prison for practically destroying our house when the divorce happened. My mom then remarried an alcoholic who left our family cold turkey when I was 17 years old. He left behind two daughters, my half sisters. They were two and eight at the time. All these things were going through my mind as I laid on the top bunk in a cell with other inmates downtown in the holding center. I remember trying not to let the other inmates hear me as I cried. I still wonder if they heard me or not, but they never said anything. Either way, I was so upset that my childhood wasn't different. I played the blame game and felt sorry for myself. I was later convicted as a felon and did 6 months of weekends. That's where you literally drove yourself to jail every Friday and drove yourself home on Sunday evenings. I called them my "Weekend Get Aways." They weren't exactly get-aways though, more like "Lock Aways." I spent my 22nd birthday in a jail cell that weekend. Of course, it landed on a Saturday. Fourth of July landed on a Saturday that year, as well. And of course, it was during the summer months, so I missed every fun activity that summer, staring at white walls and out a barred window. I missed the cabin parties my friends threw. I missed all the beach camp fires. I missed the family get-togethers, the birthday parties, etc. I remember watching the fireworks from Fourth of July in the distance through the window saying to myself that I would never let this happen to me again.

It really wasn't as bad as it sounds. It taught me a few valuable lessons. I realized that no one could ever again make me so angry that I would want to end up back in the slammer. It made me realize that most men were in there for doing the same exact thing over and over again. I learned to learn from mistakes. I made some temporary friends and learned how to play cards. I learned some street smarts, and I had a free costume for Halloween that year since I stole my uniform the last weekend I served. That was illegal, but I didn't care at the time. My then girlfriend was a cop for Halloween that year, and everyone thought it was funny. Remember my poison? *Performance*.

While serving my weekends, I started working at a marketing company, selling knives. Hey, I needed a job, and who would have hired a convicted felon? To my advantage, the application didn't ask if I was a felon. Don't ask, don't tell. I turned out to be really good at sales, I guess. I was number one that year in the office in sales, and I was promoted to be an assistant manager the first five months I worked there. I eventually learned how to run interviews, training, meetings, etc. At the age of 22, I was handed the keys to run an office for the marketing company in another city in the state. I was getting good at this performance thing, and I liked it. I was my own boss; I was an entrepreneur and was running the show at my very own office. We did well that year. We broke the previous ten-year record in sales for the office and then nearly doubled it the next year. I was saving everything I made, and I was making six figures at the age of 24. I was promoted back to Buffalo, NY to run the office I was interviewing for two years earlier. I read every self-help book I could get my hands on and even read 50 books in a year, while working at least 60 hours a week every single week I worked. I didn't mind because my performance ego was being fueled; therefore, I never ran on empty. I was able to take my mom to Hawaii, my brother to South America, and my sister to Germany and Hungary. I paid for all the trips. I bought a house. Had a summer and winter car. I had a college fund for my nephew. I was single and felt like Brad Pitt. I was going on 4-5 vacations a year, paid for by the company. I think you get the idea.

It Was Never Enough.

I remember the first time it hit me that it was never going to be enough. I was 24 years old, and we were coming off our best year ever as an office. We doubled the previous record the year before. I was on top of the world. I was really happy. I realized I was going to get several awards at the year-end banquet for our company. I never received an award as a kid unless you want to count a participation ribbon. I was excited, and I wanted my dad to be proud. My dad wasn't legally allowed to see me until I was 14 years old. He wanted to be in my life and make up for lost time, but like most of us, we struggle and tend to hurt others, when we don't even realize it. I called my dad to invite him to the year-end banquet for our company. I wanted him to come to watch me collect the awards for all my hard work the past two years. I worked tirelessly and obsessively to get to where I was at the moment. I hadn't won too many awards up to that point besides some sales awards, and I was finally getting recognized in the company as a rising star. I just needed him to show up and watch me get the awards. I told him I would pay for the hotel, the ride, and meals. I just wanted him there. My father said he didn't want to go. I asked why, and all he said was, "I just don't feel like going." I was crushed. What hurt even more was that my brother graduated from boot camp in Chicago, IL a year and half earlier. He had just joined the Navy that year after being sick of working at a dead-end job. After he finished boot camp, a six-week training, my dad drove all the way from Buffalo, NY to Chicago, IL to see his ceremony. A ten-hour drive. He paid for his own hotels, meals, and even all of our dinner that evening. No discredit to my brother's training at all. He went through hell, but that was six weeks. I worked for two years, night and day, and offered to pay for his meals, hotel, everything and even drive him. He had no interest at all of being there. The way he responded was as if I asked him to drive five hours to just have a cup of coffee with him. It took me a long time to forgive my dad for that. Forgiveness doesn't mean it didn't hurt me or affect me. It doesn't mean it was okay because it wasn't. It just means to me that I understand why he couldn't, and I don't hold it against him anymore. I love my father, and we all go through things. Some more than others. We can't give what we don't have, and if we are struggling with loving ourselves, we can very rarely give love to others, especially when we "don't feel like it." My father and I now have a good relationship, and I have forgiven him for everything. He is deeply loved, and he has an amazing purpose for his life. Nothing in his past can hold him back as long he knows that in his heart.

I eventually grew tired of the grind because, just like any poison, if we drink enough of it, we will eventually expire. I realized a few years later, at 26 years old, that it would never be enough. If I did a million dollars in sales that year, they would want 1.2 million the next year. I don't blame them. All good companies want to grow, but money wasn't a motivator for me anymore. I wasn't growing anymore, and I grew content. Too content for my liking. In my heart, I knew God had something bigger for me. I just had no clue what. I mean, it's not like I could go apply for jobs, remember? I had a felony and no college degree. I had a pretty sick resume, but most people won't hire someone with a record AND no degree. And quite frankly, I didn't want to work for anyone anyways. I hate being told what to do, and I didn't want to work a 9-5 job. I knew there was more, but more of what?

Like the lost cause I was, I left the company anyways. I broke up with my girlfriend, and then two weeks later, I broke up with my office. I didn't even plan it until one day I just sat in my office at my desk and said, "I don't want to do this anymore." I went to the property owner and asked out of my lease that morning. He let me out of the lease surprisingly. I went to my receptionist and gave her two-weeks' pay. I didn't want to do this anymore, and she totally understood. She could tell I wasn't happy anymore. I called my division manager and told him I was done. He was disappointed but accepted it. And then I realized at that moment, I had no employment and a house and two cars to pay for with no plan. What did I just do?

Destiny

It's funny how things work out when we take it one next step at a time. I told some immediate family what I did, and they thought I was nuts. Why would I walk away from a business that gave me everything I had with no plan in terms of what I was doing next? I mean, I thought I was nuts, and I quite frankly didn't understand what I was doing either. But I knew it was my next step. Sometimes, we know what we should do, but we just don't do it. It doesn't make sense logically, but we know it's the right thing to do if we want to walk into greater freedom and purpose in our lives. This was one of those times for me.

I gave God a month. I know that sounds weird, but that's what I said to myself. If I don't have anything at all by 30 days, I will unfortunately start applying for jobs and accept one of them. Two weeks went by, and I had no clue what I was doing. I wrote a resume anyways because I was bored. I applied for jobs because I was bored, but I didn't take them seriously. I knew it wasn't what was planned for me. I saw on social media my friend was working for a publishing company, and I knew a couple other old colleagues that left the marketing company I once worked for and were now franchise owners. Long story short, I inquired, and I was accepted as a franchise owner for the publishing company in Buffalo, NY. The only catch was that we had make 40 sales before we got paid as a franchise owner. I'm skipping a lot of details as to why, but that's the story in a nutshell. Forty sales and you get paid. They said it took the average person four to six months to get to 40 sales, and fifty percent of people who do get hired don't make it. Keep in my mind, I have a mortgage and bills, and I live on my own. I felt God was calling me to this even though I wasn't motivated by money anymore. I just felt like this was it, so I flew to Chicago for training and discovered that the company was a biblically-based company. I had no idea when I accepted the position. That was so God.

They called the race to 40 sales our "Ramp Up" period as franchise owners. I want to mention that even though to a lot of people this would have been nerve wrecking, I wasn't really that nervous. I knew I could do it as hubris as that may sound, and as I sat in the room with 40 other franchisees with me being one of the youngest in there by about 10 years, I would've bet on myself before anyone else. I knew I had the work ethic, tenacity, and drive to succeed in anything I put my mind to and that I wanted. I knew this because of the prior experience of seeing myself work so hard for everything. What I'm trying to say is that ***my previous next steps paved the way for my next step.*** And even though I stayed a little too long at the marketing company, it made me ready for my next step. I was officially off to the races in my "ramp up" period as a franchise owner after borrowing a lot of money from my brother and my mom to keep myself afloat during ramp up. I got my 40 sales in three months, not without a hitch, of course. I was arrested two times during ramp up for driving on a suspended license because I couldn't pay my old parking tickets. I didn't have enough money to pay my car payments, so my car was repossessed. I lied to my girlfriend that my car was in the shop that weekend. Not my finest moment. My mom had to pay what I owed to get my car back. I remember the second time I was arrested for driving on a suspended license. My mom had to come pick me up and drive my car home since I couldn't legally do so. As soon as my mom parked my car in my driveway, I took the keys and got back in the car. My mom asked me what I was doing, and I told her that I needed to get 40 sales so I could make this all worth it. She was floored and afraid of me being arrested again. I drove to my next appointment and made a sale. I never made so many phone calls and worked so hard in a short time period in my life as I did during ramp up. I was also in a very unhealthy relationship at the time that I didn't have the energy to end because of what I was going through. It was so stressful at times, but there were very few moments in my life that I felt more empowered than in those ramp up months. I knew I wasn't alone, and I knew this was part of my journey. Have you ever felt so sure of what you were supposed to do even though it didn't make sense to others? Even though it seemed chaotic and messy, you knew this was a storm you needed weather? This was one of those moments for me.

As I said, I eventually got through ramp up and paid everyone back immediately. I now make more money than I ever have in my life, and I have never felt so free. Not because of the income but because when I look back at it all, it was never really about one big step for me. It was being bold enough to take my next step and finding out more of who I was and what I was created to do. I now have the time and financial freedom to speak to college students across the country and share my story. I am now able to take my next step to empower students and help them take their next steps. I am now able to take a next step at this moment and write this book. My journey was never about one next step. It was about taking one next step every single day. It was about taking next steps to know more of who I am and what I was created to do and then doing it in that moment. It was never about achieving something or hitting a goal even though that is great, as well. It was about walking INTO my destiny every day. I am all about goals, planning ahead, and working for what you want. I set goals, and I plan ahead. I just don't place my identity and victory in those things anymore.

I think the wrong question we can sometimes ask ourselves is "What is my destiny?" I think the right question is "What is my next step?" Which one is more empowering and specific? Which one creates more action? My destiny was never a destination or even a goal I could achieve. Life is actually about taking my next step every day that brings greater freedom and purpose. For me, it's about walking with Jesus and seeing what next step He has for me, whether it's forgiving someone that has hurt me, discovering more of who I am, or even facing something head on because I need to heal from a past wound. It's not just about achieving another goal for me. Goals are great, and we need those sometimes to get things done. I have goals every year and post them around my house. I love goals, but I don't put my identity in them. There will always be more goals and more things to achieve. For me I want to be more than a conqueror.

Who We are Becoming is More Important Than What We are Doing.

When we know who we are, we naturally just do those things. I love how Pastor John Stickl at my church describes it. A cow moos, a dog barks, a cat meows, a bird flies, a fish swims. But how weird would it look if a fish tried to live its life as a cow? As obnoxious as that sounds, I see a lot of us trying to do the same thing. We are trying to do and achieve something outside of our design. We try to achieve so we can become someone. We try to be someone that others want us to be. We try to imitate, but we are only fooling ourselves and weighing ourselves down. Some of us can try to keep ourselves busy so we don't have to feel what's going wrong in our lives or hearts, but when we know who we are, the doing will just naturally happen. We don't need to tell a cat to meow, a fish to swim, or a bird to fly. They just do it because they know who they are and what they were created to do. How many of us are trying to be a bird that barks because the world is telling us we need to be something else? Is that true for you?

This was revolutionary for me because I was trying to achieve and perform so I could become someone. If I make enough people laugh, make enough money, go on enough vacations, or break enough records, I would become someone worth emulating. For others, it might be if I drink enough drinks, do enough drugs, work enough hours, or do enough of this hobby, I will finally be someone worth loving or emulating. I would then become significant. I've learned that if I need the praise of people, I would fall when it wasn't there anymore. I needed to get off that rollercoaster ride. Do you?

We Can't Give What We Don't Have.

I hope you are understanding this. When I know I am loved, I will naturally love people. When I know how much grace I've needed in my life, I will naturally give grace to others. When I know I am already significant, I will naturally do significant things not to become someone but because I already am someone. This isn't about trying harder. This isn't about doing more. This is about receiving a gift we were already given. We just need to unwrap it and willingly receive it.

This is what Jesus has done for me and has done for you. This is so hard for me to type because I hate preaching to people. I would rather just naturally live it out and let people see it for themselves. I would rather speak only for myself. Just like so many others, I just want people to show me and not tell me. Talk is cheap. But this is a book, and I may never meet you in person. I hate when people preach to me and tell me what to do. So this is the last thing I want to do to you. But I just can't tell you my story without telling you this truth in my life.

You may believe in karma, fate, or some other higher power with a purpose for your life, which is everyone's choice to make. As for me, that higher power is Jesus Christ.

Because of Jesus, I am working from victory, not for it. Because of Jesus, I am already a beloved son of a good Father (God); therefore, I can love others and work from love. I was already forgiven for everything I've done wrong; therefore, I can freely forgive others and not get offended so easily. This does not mean I'm perfect because I am far from it. But it was never about being perfect but following the One who was perfect (Jesus). I am empowered every day because of Jesus' grace in my life. Otherwise, I would be tied down by my failures and missed opportunities. I would be so stressed because I would need to work for my identity and status versus just receiving it. Because of all this truth, I am able to take my next steps every single day and awaken into my destiny one next step at a time. It was never about doing all these things and performing. It was about becoming who I already was, a beloved son who is ready to release love and hope into a broken world. Jesus never needed anything from me.

He just wants everything for me. Everything I just said is available to you, yes, you. This isn't something for you achieve but just to receive in your heart. This isn't about your past. This is about your present and future. Heaven isn't a destination to somewhere someday if we are religious enough or follow enough rules. It's something to experience today. Every time we release and receive what God has for us, we are literally bringing heaven down to earth and releasing his kingdom. I hope this makes sense to you. In other words, we can have joy and life today, not someday. For me, it's not about following rules or a religion. I actually don't even like the word *religion*. For me, it's about receiving from a relationship with someone. And that someone is Jesus. It was also never about *doing*. It was about *receiving*. And the doing just naturally happens. When a bird knows it's a bird, it just flies. Maybe this is your next step. To receive what Jesus has to offer.

I Hated Church Growing Up.

If you are anything like me you grew up going to church because you had to. I grew up Roman Catholic. I never wanted to go to church growing up. It was boring and smelled like old people. I never felt better when I went to church. I had to be silent for an hour and that was very hard for me. I remember sneaking into my mom's room to turn off her alarm clock so we would miss church. I think you get the idea. I wanted nothing to do with it and I didn't understand it. It just felt like rule following and I wasn't very good at that. Once I turned 17 my mom said I didn't have to go anymore. I was relieved and didn't look back. Not until I was 23. I feel like most people meet Jesus at their lowest point. I met Him at my highest point. I met him at the pinnacle of my success. Like I said before I just knew it was never going to be enough. So, I did my research on my own, read books and reached out to a pastor named Leroy. A year later I went on a mission's trip and my walk with Jesus grew one next step at a time. That was the turning point for me.

Struggle

Even though I follow Jesus, I openly admit I can still struggle with some things. I can struggle with purity in my relationship with my current girlfriend. We have been dating for over a year, and we have remained pure in our relationship. I was pure in my last relationship, as well. As a young guy who didn't grow up with that in my early '20s, I've struggled to stay with that. I couldn't have been the furthest thing away from staying pure in my early to mid-twenties. I've always struggled with lust. I've been addicted to pornography and can still struggle with it. I used women to make myself feel better and to make me feel like a man. I have next steps to take. When I see someone struggling, I am reminded that we all can struggle with something. Some are just more public than others and or we can just mask it better than the next person. I have seen some things happen in my life I wish it didn't happen, like my friend Stephen tragically dying so young. I didn't understand it and still don't.

I don't understand everything, but I do know I make a terrible God. I've tried to take control of every aspect of my life, and it was exhausting. I know life with Jesus and without. I choose Jesus every time, and because I follow the greatest leader of all time, I am now a great leader. And so are you. I've learned great leaders are great followers.

Sometimes our next step is the hardest one to take. Next Steps usually aren't easy to take. They often make us suck up our pride or admit we were wrong. But they free us the more we take them. But sometimes we need to go through valleys to get to the top of the mountain. Sometimes we need to be grateful for the valleys so we can be grateful when we reach the top. We can't always have the highs without the lows, and I know that If I want to experience everything God has called me to do in my life, I need to take my next steps, not because He needs me to but because there is more in it for me than just staying where I am. It was never about religion for me. It was about discovering more of who I am and what I was created to do and then doing that. There is so much more for us when we take next steps instead of staying put. Staying put and playing it safe are only affecting you and those around you, not God. We are as close to God as we want to be, and we are as free as we allow ourselves to be.

You see, I can't brag about anything that I have in my life. I can sit here and try to brag about how talented I am, but who gave me the talent? Not me. I can say, "Well, I took advantage of all the opportunities in my life. I'm a self-made man." But who gave me the opportunities? Not me. I might be able to say I took advantage of every day in my life, but who gave me life each day? I have been given so much in my life, and I can't brag about any of it.

Questions

When you hear the word *destiny*, what comes to mind?

When was there a time in your life when you took a next step, despite apathy of others?

What next step do you feel in your heart you need to take right now?

When are you going to take that next step?

What do you feel like you need to receive so you can naturally give it?

Your story is worth being told. What's your story?

Chapter 2: Next-Step Leaders (Taking Next Steps So Others Can Take Theirs.)

Next-Step Leaders aren't entirely focused on others' next steps. They are focused on their next steps. When did leading become just telling people what to do? And I know we hear that leaders are servants, and we lead by example. You've probably heard that philosophy, but where do you actually see it happening? It starts with us. What if we stopped focusing on what's wrong with others and started focusing more on what's wrong with us? What if we stopped judging others and how un-perfect they are and realize we aren't any better in the end?

As Leaders, We Teach What We Know, but We Reproduce Who We Are.

What I'm trying to say is that next step leaders aren't about inspiring just through words. They are about action within themselves. They are consistently taking next steps so others can take theirs. If we aren't growing, we are creating an environment of stagnation, apathy, and entitlement. There is no middle ground. You see, when we start looking at what we have done versus what next step we are taking, pride can start to set in. We can start to feel entitled, and entitled people rarely take next steps, not good ones anyways. I'll at least speak for me. When I started feeling like I "arrived" when I ran an office for a marketing company, I stopped taking next steps. I felt like I had nothing else to learn, really. I felt like I'd mastered everything. I didn't, but I felt like I had. I won some awards, took home some trophies, and was ready to coast off my present knowledge and success. I then lost energy to do the little things right. I started delegating where I shouldn't have. I took shortcuts where I knew I could; I totally lived off my past knowledge and credentials. I shrugged off the hard conversations and ignored them, when possible. Not having energy as leaders makes cowards out of us. We don't do the hard things anymore. At least I didn't.

Slowly but surely my office staff started to become resentful. They were pulling all the weight as I did the bare minimum. They didn't say it at first since I was the man in charge, but they showed it in their actions and how they treated their coworkers. Eventually they spoke up and didn't want to do my hard chores anymore. Sales went down, retention went down, morale went down, and people stopped caring. Why? Because I stopped. I told myself I didn't need to do the little things anymore. I felt as if I didn't need to learn, so others followed suit that were under me. I was no longer taking next steps but merely trying to coast off past accomplishments. Sometimes our actions are speaking so loudly people around us can't hear us anymore.

I see it too often today. People staying at the same job for 20 years but haven't learned anything new the past five years. They try to avoid any change. Some people have ten years of experience on paper, but they really have the same one year of experience ten times over. And what does that enable the rest of the people in the environment to do? Do the least and try to gain the most. Maybe this sounds familiar to you? It sounds familiar to me. I was that leader for a total of two years. A stagnant leader versus a next-step leader. I've read the servant leader books. I read probably over 100 books on leadership before all this happened. So, what was the problem? I wasn't reading or growing anymore. All that reading and learning was a couple years earlier, when I was taking next steps. I wasn't growing; therefore, I was dying, in my career field anyways. You see, the less we grow the more we think about ourselves. Our pities, our downfalls, what's wrong versus what's right. We focus on the problems versus trying to find real solutions. We take shortcuts versus doing things the right way. We start caring more about ourselves versus others. I finally realized my problem and shut down my office. I'd had enough of being stagnant. That was scary because I had no place to go, but I knew it was my next step. And sometimes pain is the best teacher. I was no longer growing or taking next steps. I needed change, and sometimes a change of environment that even we put ourselves in is what's best for us.

When We Take Next Steps, We Create Space so Others can Take Theirs.

I wasn't growing as a leader, so others didn't have a chance to either. Just like a fish will stop growing when their fish tank is too small, we rarely, I mean rarely, outgrow our environments. If you are the best person in the room in terms of growth and taking next steps for a long time, you probably should upgrade your environment or sphere of influence. As I mentioned earlier, great leaders are great followers, as well. They are keenly aware of their environment and who they surround themselves with. Next-Step Leaders are aware of the energy and environment in their lives, and they put guardrails on them. No point in ending up in a ditch if we can first be stopped by a guardrail.

So, when we are passionate about our people and what we are creating, I want you remember that every next step you are taking in your own life is creating space for others to take theirs, not just in your work or organization, but in your personal life. Your family, your friends, your significant other. This isn't an organizational leadership tool; this is a lifestyle of helping others while you're helping yourself.

I Want You to Ask Yourself this Hard Question.

Do you even want to take a next step where you are in your organization or personal life? How about in your relationship? Do you feel the need or passion to want to keep taking next steps? If not, maybe it's time to move on then. Maybe you've heard it before: *if you aren't growing you are dying.* I believe in that. There is no neutral. We are either growing or moving backwards every day. You see we can't grow where we don't want to grow. We can't force ourselves. We can't always make our fish tank bigger.

As leaders, we must be intentional with everything we are doing. We act and live with purpose. And not just be busy for the sake of being busy (more on that in another chapter). We can't just go where we feel important and wanted. We must go where we are needed as next-step leaders. That includes our family, our kids, our significant others, or even people that just need a good mentor.

One Dimensional Leader

Don't be a one-dimensional leader where you are good at one thing and ignore another important part of your life. I've been that leader, where I was a great leader in an organization, but I ignored my significant other. I gave her the scraps of what was left of my day. I gave her what was left over and put her in my schedule where she could fit. Then one day, she told me how she felt, and I had a choice to make. Either way, I had a next step to take. A next step to make her a priority or a next step to realize that I didn't want to make her a priority. There was no wrong answer because not making a decision is still a decision. It's just not a good one. Next-Step Leaders don't ignore hard questions. I decided to make my schedule fit around when she needed me. We are a team, and I didn't want to be one of those leaders that had a great work life and an emotionless, meaningless life at home. I didn't want to be one of those dads in the future. I didn't want to be one of those future husbands. You see, I am not married, and I am not a dad. We can't make changes after those opportunities arrive. We need to be aware of who we are becoming so when those next steps do come, we already took other next steps to become who need to be: someone amazing and ready for the next chapter in our life. As a leader, don't wait for opportunities to get ready for them. Mold yourself now by taking next steps so when that next chapter comes up, you are already prepared. Don't wait when you're supposed to move. Don't be a one-dimensional leader.

What Are YOU Promoting as a Leader?

I'm not sure if you've noticed yet, but we haven't mentioned that you need a title to be a leader or a next-step leader. Most people look for ability. God looks availability. My question is this: are you available? I'm going to assume you aren't aware and just tell you that you don't need a title to lead. We are all leaders one way or another. We are all leading something or someone. We are leading others through our actions every day. We are either leading our friends into apathy, or we encouraging them to grow through our actions. Who we are and what we are doing are promoting something. What are you promoting? What are you promoting as a friend, a coworker, or a significant other? Most people promote gossip, slander, or what's wrong with situations. Most people talk about what's wrong with people and why things should be better without offering an action to help. Please don't be one of those people. They are leaders but not ones we want to follow.

What We Tolerate, We Promote.

I used to think, if I didn't participate in something, then I wasn't a part of it. For example, if there is a group message bad-mouthing someone, and I don't respond, then it's okay. I mean, I didn't chip in the conversation, so it doesn't matter, right? Wrong. *What we tolerate is what we promote.* If we tolerate gossiping in our circle of friends, we are promoting it. Why? Because we are involved with what we tolerate. I'm not saying to start a fight on social media or in the middle of your friends. Maybe just removing ourselves from the group text works, or simply stating that we should change the subject when the other person we are talking about is around is a great friendly way to redirect the conversation. Talking one-on-one usually works best for me. You see, I don't have a solution for every circumstance, and that's not even what I want to focus on. I don't want myself or even you to focus on what you are doing. I want you to focus on who you are becoming. Who we are becoming is more important than what we are doing. Once we know who we are and what we stand for, the doing just naturally happens. As a leader, I don't want to be around people who just build themselves or even amuse themselves by bringing others down. Therefore, I either redirect it or remove myself from those people. It makes it very clear that I don't want to be around that. I also want to say this because it makes my heart healthier. When I tolerate something, I don't want to be a part of, not only am I promoting it, but I am also affecting my heart as a leader. Faith comes by hearing and what we hear our faith grows in. Just listen to what people listen to on the radio and then see their actions follow. I can't focus on helping others when I'm listening to Kesha sing about drinking a bottle of Jack in the morning. Get my drift? What are you tolerating in your life?

Leaders Are NOT Perfect.

I remember the first time I was so disappointed in a leader. He was my leader, and I thought so well of him for years. He was charismatic, very well liked, friendly, did nothing wrong, and did so well in our industry.

I was at a conference in San Diego, and it was the first time I was ever on a plane at the ripe age of twenty-three. I seriously had never been on a plane until I was 23 years old. It was also my very first leadership conference as an entrepreneur running my own office. I had two assistant managers I hired that summer running the office while I was gone at the conference. I was also planning on staying in San

Diego another week after the conference since my twin brother was stationed in San Diego for his service in the Navy at the time. I was excited for my first trip and first vacation since becoming a business owner.

Then, it all came crashing down before dinner one night at the conference. I received a phone call from my assistant manager that he couldn't run the office while I am gone anymore because he hasn't paid his car insurance in months and can't drive to the office. He also lived an hour away, so walking or hitching a ride everyday was nearly impossible. My other assistant manager was away at college during this time, so I had no reserves ready to take his place. I was stuck and in a panic as a real first problem running an office. Who would let the receptionists in? Who would pay them? Who would run interviews and training and make sure all the sales reps were working? I immediately went to my division manager for help. To his credit, we were having dinner on an old war ship in San Diego, and it was pretty dang cool. The guy is a war fanatic and was excited to check it out. I tried to tell him my scenario while my assistant was on the phone. I asked for his help, and he immediately dismissed me, telling me he would be right back. I waited there for ten minutes, realizing he wasn't coming back. I never felt so alone in a problem before. Anger and resentment built up in me that day for that person even though I never admitted it. I actually liked the guy and thought he was an awesome leader. But I never understood at the time and years after that why he would blow me off so quickly when I was in such need of his advice and help. It took me 4-5 years before I finally forgave him. He probably had no idea now that I think about it. I'm laughing as I write this. Leaders aren't perfect. Accept it and move on. I am 100% sure I have done worse and then some. Leaders are people; people are human, and humans make mistakes. We can't put our identity and our ability to lead in the hands of others or how they always treat us. We are responsible for ourselves in the end, and making excuses on how others have treated us as leaders is a waste of time. You might have been hurt by a leader, and I am so sorry that happened to you. Things can be really difficult, and leaders have the responsibility to handle those situations differently than they do sometimes. If we are focused on things we can't control, those things can hinder us from taking next steps. Remember, we take next steps because it brings us into greater freedom and purpose.

I'm Not a Perfect Leader.

I want to end this chapter with telling you how imperfect I am. Seriously. My point of this is to encourage you. I've made more mistakes than I want to admit as a leader. I've delegated way too much in the past. I've manipulated to get out of hard situations. I've taken advantage of my power as a leader. I've used it for the wrong things. I have created environments of apathy with my leadership. I've tolerated gossip and even spread it myself plenty of times. I didn't seek mentors that were well-rounded. I've created a façade of how I have everything together, and I've tried to teach other's how to do the same thing. What a waste of time for others and myself. I don't have everything together every single day. I've failed others and even family members as a leader.

I remember my cousin who used to work for me as a sales rep. I remember him looking up to me and even telling his friends how much of the "Real Deal" I was. He was around 17 years old. When he was finally old enough to work for me, he did. In fact, he was in my training on his 18th birthday, and I was 25 years old, I believe it was about five years ago. I remember I was coming off my best year ever as an office in sales. I was making six figures a year for the second year in a row, and I just turned twenty-five. I remember how awesome I thought I was, and I'm kind of embarrassed to admit that now, If I'm being honest. I remember letting him down as a cousin and as a leader. I was sleeping around with some of the sales reps in the office, even though I promoted we don't do that as a team. I remember taking short cuts as a leader because I felt entitled. I remember feeling like an awesome manager on the outside, but I knew deep down I wasn't the leader I needed to be. I was a fraud on the inside but looked great on the outer layer. The leaders I built up that year realized sooner or later I wasn't who I was promoting. I ran the leadership academy that year and just went off what I did the year before curriculum-wise. No preparation really and just went with whatever happened. That was a recipe for disaster, and I lost the respect of others and unfortunately my cousin. That hit me harder than any of the others. Family means everything to me.

I say all this to say that, if you've felt any of those feelings, I've been there. I've been the fraud. I've been the person who tries to make it look great on the outside without worrying about what's underneath. I've taken the shortcuts, and I fell into what I desired at the moment. I was more focused on what I was doing versus who I was becoming. Sometimes we try to use old steps to take next steps, and I ran out of stairs.

I am so thankful that we don't have to be perfect to lead because I could have given up right there. I'm so thankful my past doesn't have to be my future. Grateful doesn't even begin to describe how thankful I am to get to walk in freedom and not shame every day. I am driven by Jesus' grace, not past expectations or past failures. Jesus loves us too much to keep us where we are. I can focus on my next step as a leader, working from love, not for it-not from my missteps-and so can you! If you aren't perfect, join the club, and you are in good company. I'm not here to say what I did was okay. It wasn't. But I'm not worried about my past anymore; I don't live there. Next-Step Leaders walk in freedom, taking one next step at a time, and they can walk step-by-step into their destiny. Our past experiences are not our future expectations.

Questions

What's a next step for you to take as a leader?

What are you promoting or tolerating? Both good and bad.

Are you creating an environment for others to grow in?

Do you consider yourself a leader?

If the world followed you around for a day, would they better for it?

Do you see others taking next steps on a consistent basis?

Next-step Leaders have healthy hearts full of grace and love. Is your heart healthy?

Chapter 3: Gratitude A Next Step We All Should Take

I've borrowed money from people and haven't been paid back. Trust has been broken. I've had things stolen from me. I've been taken advantage of plenty of times in different situations. My time has been wasted. My schedule and time have been taken for granted. I've been lied to. I've been hurt. My heart has been broken. I'm sure you probably can relate to these things, some more than others. But what keeps me going? Being grateful.

Here's how I look at it -

I'm thankful I even have time to waste. My life isn't insured every day.

I'm thankful that I had money to give even though it has been stolen.

I'm thankful I've had my dad for 16 years versus the 14 years I didn't have him. I'm more thankful for the good he has done versus the not so good he has done. I mean wouldn't you want people to see you in the same light? I know I do. I'm thankful the people closest to me see me like Jesus does. They see me for who I am becoming versus who I wasn't.

I'm really grateful I had an open heart because, even though an open heart can feel a lot of pain, it can love like a closed heart never can. I'm thankful for the bad because I can experience the good.

For the times my trust has been broken, I've also been shown that I can trust others and expect the good in people.

And for some odd reason, I've always felt that if someone steals something from me, it's probably because they needed it more than I did. My significant other, however, doesn't think that's a good reason to leave the car unlocked in the driveway.

See the Gift

I remember when I first got my hunting license. I was 19 years old. And I remember my dad being so excited to go hunting with me and pass along tips and knowledge that he has learned over the years. If you want to catch my dad's attention, bring up hunting and be prepared to listen a long time. Whether you are listening or not, he keeps going.

I remember going buck hunting my first hunting season. It wasn't what I fully expected. During shotgun season in Buffalo, NY, it gets really cold. My dad likes to get to the tree stand before its light out, so we are up at 4 a.m. easily. I am not exactly a morning person that wakes up super early easily. I also don't like being cold, so to wake up super early and to be cold just sounds like no fun for me. So on the weekends on my days off at 19 years old, I was doing the exact opposite of what I wanted. I didn't want to wake up early, and I definitely didn't want to be cold. And when we did finally get into the tree stand, we just sat there. And I mean we just sat there and stared into the dark woods. We couldn't talk. We couldn't move really. And for someone who has ADHD, that is the last thing I wanted to do. My dad also wouldn't let me bring my cell phone.

I think you see that I felt like I made a mistake pretty quickly if I wanted to do what I wanted to do. I wanted to have fun on the weekends with my then girlfriend and friends. I wanted to stay up late and hang out with everyone, but here I was going to bed at 9 p.m. and waking up early to trek out into the wilderness in the middle of nowhere and freeze my butt off. If I fell asleep in the tree stand, I would have fallen to my probable death. I also had to pay for a hunting license, which took one of my weekly paychecks for washing dishes that week. Woot woot!

I did that for the next two or three years. Why? Because it made my father happy. It was the time we got to share together uninterrupted. Growing up with other siblings and living in a fast-paced world, I wanted to make up time that I lost with him. But more importantly and the biggest reason? It was for him. When I got my first 8-point buck, I'm pretty sure my dad was way more excited than I was. He was a kid in a candy store with a hundred dollars. The gift in the whole situation was that I got to spend time with my dad and make an impact on our relationship. Even though it doesn't make up for the time we missed, we made memories that we couldn't make any other way. We were sharing his passion and what he loved. In those moments, I learned there is a gift in every situation we face, despite circumstances. There is always something to be grateful for.

I'm not thankful I beat up some guy when I was 20 years of age, but I am thankful I was arrested and did six months of weekends. It was a wake-up call that I needed, and it showed me the world didn't revolve around me. That I wasn't invincible. It's unfortunate that my dad wasn't there for my earlier years, but I am so thankful for the gift of a loving mother that did her best for me and my siblings. I am grateful for the time we have now. It's unfortunate that I have a record for the rest of my life, but I'm thankful that I have an opportunity to be my own boss and not work for anyone. My record makes me pursue my dreams since I can't pass a background check for a regular job.

For the unhealthy relationships, I can focus on wasted time or what I learned. I recognize mistakes I won't make again and unhealthiness in myself and a potential significant other. I am thankful for realizing my flaws so I could fix them. It gave me the courage to wait for the right person. Unfortunately, again sometimes pain is the best teacher in our lives. That is sometimes the gift since we couldn't learn it any other way. At least it was for me. Pain can be a gift.

For every mishap in my life, there was a gift in every situation. Where are your gifts in the unfortunate events in your life? What about right now in your life, in this very moment?

I'll be Happy When...

I used to tell myself when I was younger that, once I achieved certain goals or dreams, I would finally be happy. Or to dive in a little deeper, I thought, once I achieved a certain status in my life, I would worth being loved and emulated. I was even trying to impress people that I didn't really like or care to have a real relationship with. I used to fool myself with "I would be happy when…" and then fill in the blank.

I feel like we can all be caught up in the "I'll be happy when" theory.

It might look something like this:

I'll be happy when this semester is finished.

I'll be happy when I finally graduate from college.

I'll be happy once I get a job in my field.

I'll be happy when get a raise.

I'll be happy when I meet someone who loves me for me.

I'll be happy once I'm married.

I'll be happy when I have kids.

I'll be happy once the kids start going to school so I can have more free time.

I'll be happy once the kids move out.

I'll be happy when I retire.

I'll be happy once we go on that dream vacation.

The list can go on and on. I think you see where I am going with this. The problem with how we are made up is that we will always want more, and it will never truly fully be enough. We are conditioned to always want more.

I've found out, at least for myself, that if I'm not joyful in this exact very season of my life I won't be later. If I don't have a heart full of gratitude now, I won't be for long later.

Where Does Your Identity Come From?

To get to the point, this comes down to identity for me. Where do I get my joy and gratitude from? Where do you? Why should I be grateful for where I am when I'm not where I want to be? Doesn't that fuel my energy to always keep going after what I want? To achieve more? Absolutely, and there is nothing wrong with goals and wanting more. In fact, I encourage it. But I couldn't put my identity in my goals anymore and what I had achieved. You see, my poison was performance, and I realized it was never going to be good enough. If I wasn't grateful for where I am now, I won't be later.

I also realized things are most likely always going to change.

- Relationships change (Friends, dating, etc.…)
- Money changes because people lose jobs, companies go under, and yes that residual income that you swear is fool proof can change too.
- Circumstances change

All these have changed significantly for me in my 30 years of living. And so, for me, I couldn't put my identity, gratitude, or joy in things that change. It wouldn't be healthy for me or my future family. I realized I needed to put my joy in a rock that never changes and is ever-present my whole life, despite me not realizing all the time. I put my identity, joy, and gratitude in Jesus Christ, a person whose promises never waver, grace never changes, and love can't be earned, only received. Because of Jesus, I am already forgiven and forever loved, and because of his presence in my life, I always have purpose. God is good; therefore, anything is possible. That has changed my life, and because of that, I am able to walk in freedom every day, despite circumstances. I'm not here to preach. I hate being preached at. I just can't tell my story without Jesus, not anymore at least. Everything I am and everything that I own belongs to Jesus. Therefore, I can let go of anything, and I can do anything because I partner with God every day to release love, grace, healing, and purpose into this world every day. Not because God needs me to, but because he empowers me with the same thing every day. What we receive is what we give out. If we only let in ungratefulness, we will only let out more of the same. You see, I care more about what Jesus says about me more than what people have to say about me. It was never based on what I did but what Jesus did for me and continues to do. This isn't a one-time event but truth I receive every day and so can you. This isn't something to be achieved. It can only be received. That's what so amazing about grace.

Grace, Freedom and Judgement

What are the differences between judgement, mercy, and grace?

Judgement is when you get what you deserve.

Mercy is when you don't get what you deserve.

Grace is when you get what you didn't deserve.

I remember when my friend, Ryan, and I went to Delray Beach Florida to visit my cousin, Rob. We went out that night to a taco bar, and we made a toast of being together in a beautiful city with friends and family. The guy next to us got somehow offended by our toast. I mean, it was so out of left field that it didn't make any sense to us. We were dumbfounded. The guy's wife was even confused, and the look of embarrassment was on her face as he was getting angrier and angrier as we tried to defuse the situation. My cousin, Rob, being the older cousin that he is, tried to stand up for us, but Ryan did something I didn't expect him to do. He immediately stepped in and said, "Hey I'm really sorry if we offended you at all. I will pay for your dinner and drinks for the evening." I immediately sat there and reacted like he spoke a foreign language. Why the heck would Ryan pay for a guy's dinner and drinks that was being rude, violent in a way, and flat out obnoxious? I couldn't believe it. Would you? The guy didn't deserve it. The guy, that was so angry and offended, went from angry to stunned to happy and immediately began apologizing for overreacting. He shook our hands, and we went about the rest of our night celebrating being together and experiencing Delray Beach. Wow! That's what grace does though, and that's what we can do as leaders. We can bring the opposite spirit in terrible situations, whether the situation is our fault or not. You see, grace not only forgives us when we are wrong, but it also credits our account. It doesn't just forgive us; it gives more than we deserve tenfold. Another way to say it is that grace not only forgives us, it credits our account. It pays back what we owed and then gives us more.

That is why I am so grateful. Because what Ryan did for that guy, I feel like Jesus does for me every day. He loves, doesn't judge, doesn't point out what we did wrong, and gives more than we deserve despite our flaws. That is something to only receive and not earn. It is that good. What if we received that grace every day? How different would our lives be? How much joy and life would we have? And even better, how much love, grace, and truth could we give others, even when it's not warranted?

I can show off what I've done, or I can show off how much grace I've needed. The first one brings expectations that I can probably never meet and a façade that I can never live up to. The other one brings freedom, truth into my life, and a heart of gratitude to those around me. Which one would you rather have?

So, what are you receiving every day? Do you feel grateful or ungrateful most days? Where do you see yourself putting your identity?

A good way to figure that out is time and money. Where you invest most of your time and money is where you most likely put your identity.

I don't need to meet you to see what you are all about. Just show me your calendar and your bank statement.

What does yours say about you?

Being thankful and putting my identity in Jesus has kept my heart full despite circumstances. As leaders and people taking next steps, we can change any environment we are in. Not the circumstances, but the environment and energy. We can control the thermometer in the room. We have more of a voice than we give ourselves credit for, and we can have more joy to receive than what we have been giving ourselves. Joy isn't always about adding more. In fact, it's frequently the opposite. I've been to Haiti, the poorest country in the western hemisphere of the world. I've spent a week there in villages, helping people rebuild their homes, praying for them, and helping where it was needed. This was years after the earthquake they suffered. I'm telling you, if you haven't been there, it puts things in perspective. Most don't know when they will have clean water to drink. They don't know what they are going to eat that week or if they will eat. They rely everyday on instincts to survive. I will also tell you that many of these people are the most joyful people you will ever meet. Their circumstances are terrible, and most would say their quality life is terrible. Yet they are joyful and don't complain. Why is that? Because they don't put their joy in possessions or circumstances. So why are we so quick to do the opposite? That's a great question.

Questions

What's your next step in the gratitude department?

What, where, or who do you put your identity in? Is that healthy for you?

What gifts did you not see during the most unfortunate events in your life?

How do you finish the sentence "I'll be happy when..."?

Chapter 4: Mentorship, Environments, Fish Bowls, and Guardrails. Oh My!

One of my biggest fears is that I will become complacent in my life. That I let the world and some of its negativity bog me down and stop me from taking my next steps. That I hear its apathetic roar more than God's voice. If I'm being honest, it can sometimes. I can grow complacent in my heart. I can hear what the world wants to tell me versus what God has called me to do. I can hear the voices of "it doesn't matter anyways, so stop trying so hard" and "You'll never measure up." But it's so freeing to admit that I can't do this journey on my own. That I need great men in my life to help guide me back on my path and give me some encouragement. I need men to point me to the One who has already conquered those fears and that perfect love that casts out fear. I need men to challenge me when my heart isn't right or when I'm starting to have even just a little bit of apathy in my heart. In the Bible, it says a little bit of yeast ruins the whole batch of dough. A little bit of apathy and lies we tell ourselves can stop us from taking our next steps. It can keep us from our destiny. Just like small steps lead to big progress eventually, small missteps and deciding to take the easy road instead can lead to a stagnant, numbing life. And like John Stickl said in *Follow the Cloud*, "Jesus didn't give us a new heart so we can spend our life numbing it." We need guidance, and we can't do this journey on our own. Being intentional with who we put in our lives and what environment we put ourselves into goes a long way.

I'm very intentional with my time and who I spend it with. We only have so much mental capacity in a day and a week for relationships, whether it be friends, family, or coworkers, not just our significant others. I realized this a couple years ago and started being wiser with my time and who I spent it with. I started thinking who I wanted to connect with and why. I'm always asking in a healthy way *why* I'm doing what I'm doing. A lot of times, I surprise myself with the answers. Am I connecting with that person just so I can brag about what I've done, or do I want to really connect with that person? Am I speaking about this certain subject to a crowd because it builds me up or because that's what they really need to hear? Am I pursuing this goal to build my ego up or because it aligns with who I am and want to become? Asking ourselves questions is pretty powerful if we are honest with ourselves, and we need good mentors around us to help. For me, I must be intentional with who I am, what I'm listening to, and what environment I am in. If not, I start becoming someone I don't want to be, acting how I don't want to act, and doing things in the end I simply don't want to do.

Bottom line, I just don't feel free anymore because I'm no longer being intentional, and it doesn't align with who I am. I say all that to say that having mentors and great friends has really shaped who I am.

Mentors

I remember the first time I met my very first mentor, Justin. I was interviewing for a job, and he was the boss. It was the marketing company I would eventually move up in and run my own office, as well. I had no idea at the time what job I was even interviewing for. I just needed a job as a 20 years old, who was in the process of being charged with a Felony for assault for a fight earlier that year. Justin had no idea and, since it wasn't official yet, I wasn't legally obligated to tell him. I remember him running my interview, and I was so nervous. He had a really nice suit on, looked serious, and just looked like someone who ran a tight ship. I was relieved to find out I got hired when I did. I had no idea how much of an impact that guy would have on my life at the time. When I eventually told him about my record, he didn't judge me. He knew I was a hard worker who just made a couple wrong choices back then. A lot of times people are fighting battles we know nothing about. Like Jesus, Justin didn't see me as a messy person. He just saw a person in a mess. He didn't define me for what I'd done but who I am now. I just did what I was told as a sales rep and, as people in the company told every new sales rep when they started, "Just follow the program."

I would never call myself a quick learner. I think what really propelled me to success in sales so quickly was I just implemented everything I learned so quickly. Once I gathered something that could help me, I applied it immediately and took action. Too many times, I see sales reps just take in knowledge and then not apply it. What's the point of knowing something if we aren't going to apply it? Action matters, and that's what I learned from Justin. He just did it. No excuses, no whining, no time to worry, just find the solution and move forward. I never saw Justin not "on purpose" in his business. He was a no-nonsense kind of guy. You're either on his team or you're not. And what was cool is that he respected you either way. He just wanted to keep moving forward. I wanted to be around this guy as much as I could and learn. He had no idea at the time, but I really never had someone so willing to pour into my life and teach me everything I wanted to know at the time. We all need someone to believe in us and be willing to go the extra mile for us. I finally had that person in my corner at age twenty. I just remember his assistant managers saying-and eventually as an assistant manager, I got to see him-he was at the office at 6 a.m. in the morning so he could get a good start on the day. He planned for the day and planned what he was going to say to the team. I have so much to say about the guy. Simply put, the guy just out-worked everyone, and that was why his office was tops in the company. I later found out how other managers would cut corners. I eventually saw it close up.

Many managers did enough to just get by. Not all, of course, but enough where I am so thankful that I did not get one of those managers. The wrong habits I would have picked up! I would have learned how to cut corners and probably would have done so if my manager did. I would have arrived late and left early if I saw my mentor do so. We have no idea as leaders how much of an impact we have sometimes. We can lose sight of who is watching and whose life we are impacting. I lost sight of that eventually five years later, which is why I needed to leave the company. It's a good thing for them I did since I wasn't doing anyone any good anymore. Justin and I have lost touch over the years, but we do talk here and there. I have nothing but respect for him and what he taught me. I am forever grateful. What we do as leaders matter, and he taught me that. He found some 20 year old, insecure kid on the inside, who just wanted to do something with his life, and he helped him. He showed him the way, not just told him the way. There is no way I would be here today without his guidance in the beginning. Sometimes we are taking next steps, and we have no idea. God knew who I needed to impact my life, and that was one of the many ways he led me, even when I had no idea. And He is leading you somewhere if you let Him.

Intentionality with Mentors

Every month, I have coffee or lunch with the same three guys. Some more than once. I remember hearing a podcast about a guy I looked up to, even though I'd never really had a conversation with him before. Isaac Tolpin is his name. He talked about having mentors in life and how that was a big game changer for him. He talked about not just having business mentors because we could find plenty of those. He talked about men who were just as influential and intentional with their families as they were with their business endeavors or goals. That struck me. I knew a lot of great successful people. Those aren't hard to find. But what about men who were succeeding and thriving in all parts of their life? Not just business. They had a great family life. They loved their spouse and children and actually put them first at all costs. Were they someone who took next steps consistently because they knew who they were? Were they men of faith? This was a big one for me. Did they have more of a relationship with Jesus versus more of the "let's keep the favor thing going" with God? Like they were checking in with their parole officer than wanting to hear what God had to say? I searched my contacts and found very few who had all these characteristics, were living them all, and were playing the business game higher than I was. I realized my friend, John, was one of these men. He was much older than I was, had a very successful business, and an amazing family. More importantly, he was a big man of faith and had an amazing relationship with the Lord. I have a great relationship with some of his kids and son-in-law. He was a great man of faith, and he inspires me to be a great father someday. I asked him to mentor me, and I'm so glad he accepted. We meet for lunch once a month because of our busy schedules. Being intentional is so key.

I also have a best friend, Gary, who has spoken so much life into me. Constantly and annoyingly, he asks me constantly where my heart is. I mean that in a good way. He asks how I am doing and if I'm being intentional. Gary never points me to what I am doing wrong but why I am always walking in freedom. He is a friend who has the hard conversations with me because they need to be had often. A friend isn't someone who agrees with us but tells us what we need to hear. They do it from a loving heart. Grace and Truth are both important. Good friends are hard to find. If you find one, I advise you to hold onto them and be intentional with them. I meet with him usually twice a month on his lunch breaks from work.

I have a friend and mentor named Dominic, who went blind a couple years ago. We meet for coffee usually every three weeks. He is someone who I've grown to be great friends with. We met through my girlfriend, Amber. He was a great network marketer back in his hay day. He has quite a story to tell, but just like next-step leaders, his story gets better as the years pass. We don't just talk about what he has done but more importantly what will be. We talk about a better world and how we can do our part. Dominic jokes about how he has more vision for his life than he ever did when he could see. He had a heart attack a few years ago and lost his sight. He was practically dead on the table, but God had better plans for him. They started a prayer chain literally around the world, and the doctor tried a machine in the storage room that hasn't been used in over 20 years. It was a long shot, as in less than 1% chance, but they did it for the sake of trying it. It worked and now Dominic runs a foundation called *Total Breakthrough*. It's a discipleship program that's designed to disciple new Christians. All Dominic talks about is reaching the lost and the broken. His story is amazing, but it never stopped there. How many people would have stopped after having a heart attack and going blind? Dominic has such a passion for life and people that he continues to take his next steps. I am honored to know him and for him to be a mentor in my life. He is a great reminder to me and others that if you're not dead, God is still using you. And even though we can't see where we are going often in our life, we can take next steps in faith that greater things are going to happen. I believe they will, just not the way we probably planned it. Even better.

These mentors and friends in my life are constantly pouring into me. There is no way I would be where I am and who I am without them. I constantly remind people when I'm speaking that we need great mentors in our lives. It is absolutely an essential in living a life of next steps and a life uncommon. We need someone up close and personal in our lives. Not just so we can be told where we need to corrected but because we are better when united with great mentors. We are stronger. We have someone to lean on. We have someone to bounce ideas and thoughts off of. I'll speak for myself and just flat out admit that I can't do this life on my own. I can feel the pressure sometimes. I can feel things not going my way. I can get distracted and derailed by this world. But having a great support system has helped tremendously. I want to ask - do you have a mentor? Are they where you want to be? Are they living out what they talk about? How are they with their family? Are they more empowering versus being apathetic or stagnant? Maybe your next step is getting a mentor.

We are Mentoring Others around Us Without Even Knowing It.

Back to Isaac Tolpin for a moment, the guy I talked about earlier in this chapter, and how he suggested finding mentors through a podcast he was interviewed on. Isaac has no idea how much of an impact he has had on me even though we've never had a one-on-one conversation. In fact, I'm convinced that if you brought up my name, He would be very hard pressed to remember how he knows my name. He was one of the top division managers in the marketing company I worked for at the time, and I looked up to him because of his passion for life and how different he thought about life when he spoke at conferences. I must have watched his conference wrap-up talk at least 50 times. That's how impactful it was to me, and I've never heard someone be so passionate about people. Passion is a word that gets thrown around too easily, I believe. We can fake passion when holding microphone, standing on a stage, or communicating on social media, but this guy was on fire whenever I saw him. I later found out he was a Christian, and that was one of the reasons why I even became interested in my faith.

It's funny how we sometimes think things don't matter. We think people aren't watching. People are, and they are wondering if you are for real. And I bet they are secretly hoping you are even if they don't admit it. We want authentic mentorship these days, not just another "speak here and do the opposite later" kind of leader. Can I ask you a question? If the world followed you around for a day would they be better for it? Often we think what we do doesn't matter. It does. We are pushing people in the right direction or we aren't. What are you promoting? How are you mentoring people? You might think, "Well, I don't mentor people, Dave." I have to respectfully disagree with you. Someone is watching you, and someone is learning from you every day. The only question is what are they learning? The kid in the grocery sees how we treat the cashier when something isn't priced right. They see how we wait in line. They see how patient or impatient we are. They see how we treat people. Your kids, nieces, nephews, grandkids, and second cousins see you go through life often enough that you're spreading some kind of message. What message are you spreading? We can so easily get caught up in thinking it doesn't matter. It does. And apathy is spread too often. We can break that mold one next step at a time.

Fish Bowls

A fish will never outgrow its fishbowl. As a kid I loved having a fish tank. I remember when I was 12, I asked my mom for a big fish tank for my birthday. We bought a used one from someone on craigslist that just wanted to get rid of it. I kept that thing for over fifteen years. I remember learning about fish and what to do and what not to do. Make sure the water PH Levels are good and no chlorine. I remember I couldn't mix different types of fish because some fish were more territorial than others. I couldn't put goldfish with my tropical fish. I wanted so many different types of fish in my tank, but I couldn't put them all in there.

That was a bummer when I found that out. I learned fish wouldn't grow or be healthy if I had too many fish in the tank. I wanted them to be healthy, so I did what was instructed. I had fish for the next fifteen years from junior high, to high school, through my crazy years, and even when I owned an office. I brought the fish tank with me when I opened my office and kept it there until I closed it. I was done with fish after that, but I learned something. Fish are a product of their environments. They are only as healthy as their conditions and who was around them. If one fish got sick, the others usually did. If there were too many fish, they wouldn't grow to their potential. I think you know where I am going with this. I'm going to tell you anyways.

As human beings, it's very hard for us to outgrow our environment. There are some cool stories of others doing so, but those are such rare stories, which is why they are great stories. Why make it harder on ourselves if we don't have to? We need to surround ourselves with healthy growing environments.

If you are always the most successful person in your group of peers it might be time to get a bigger fish tank, a.k.a. a new group of peers. If we are surrounded by apathetic people who usually talk more about what's wrong than what's right, we need a healthier environment. If we aren't in a fish tank that promotes next steps and unity as a group, our next step might be to remove ourselves from that group. It might be time to grow your fish tank or inspire others in your group to take their next steps.

Remember, we teach what we know, but we reproduce who we are. Next Step Leaders inspire by actions not just by words. Talk is cheap, and knowledge is not power. Implementation of knowledge is power. Thirty years ago, knowledge was power. Whoever knew more usually got promoted and achieved the most in their field. Whoever had the degree would get the job, but that's not the case as much anymore. Knowledge is plentiful today. There is probably too much information actually. When was the last time any of us went a couple days without hearing someone say, "Just google it"? Knowledge isn't what gets us ahead anymore. It's the use of knowledge and whoever applies it the quickest and most efficiently. As a leader, let's not stop at learning. Let's take action right away by taking one next step at a time. And a great way for us to keep taking next steps is making sure our environment and close sphere of influence is healthy. Don't over populate the fish tank. We think the more we have or the more we do, the better we are. It's not always true. More on that later.

Friends

I remember when I moved back to Buffalo, NY from Jamestown, NY. I was promoted to run a bigger territory because of the success I had in Jamestown. I was excited because I was coming back home, and I was ready to take my next step in a bigger territory. When I came back home, I contacted some of my old friends from previous years and started hanging out with them more often since I was home permanently. I realized quickly that I outgrew a lot of my friends, not just professionally, which I didn't care about at the time really. It was more about maturity. They were still partying hard, and that's all they really cared about. I noticed a bunch of my old friends were doing some hard drugs. It escalated from drinking and marijuana to other things since I was gone. Amazing how small things eventually turn to big things.

I realized I needed new friends, and I cut 99% of them off. It was a lonely time for me. I was working 60-70 hours a week running my office, so it isn't like I could just go out and make new friends easily. I felt like the guy from the movie, "I love You, Man." I needed some new friends. I didn't want to hang out with my sales reps because I wanted to keep things professional and didn't want to cross boundaries. Plus, I was older than 90% of them. It wouldn't have been a better crowd anyways, probably since they were all college students or high school graduates. Slowly but surely, I started gaining better friends and being more intentional about who I surrounded myself with. It wasn't easy at all, but next steps aren't easy most of the time.

Some of us have heard it so many times. "You are the average of your top five friends." It's so true though…more than ever in today's world. Who are your closest friends that you hang out with and spend the most time talking to? Are they who you want to become in terms of integrity, professionalism, and as a future parent? I'm all about having fun and not taking life too seriously. Trust me. But if our top 2-5 friends aren't becoming who we want to become as people, we need to make new friends. A fish can't outgrow its environment and it can't stay healthy if the water isn't good enough. Why would we try to do the same thing? Our life may not be at risk, but the health of our heart is. We might not be getting into trouble, but we aren't acting the way we want to act and becoming who we know deep down we want to become. If I'm honest, I can struggle with this sometimes with certain friendships. And it's not their fault. It's mine. I let it happen, and when I do, I always regret it. This is a next step I am still taking as I write this book. I've gotten 90% of it down, but I am still and will always be intentional about who I am hanging out with. I hope you hear me out on this. I don't want anything from you. I want everything for you as a reader and a friend. I don't want to take anything from you. I just want to give you tools and ideas to live a life of freedom and purpose. I'm not saying get rid of all of your friends. I'm just saying be intentional about who you spend most of your time with. And sometimes changing our environment is one of those next steps. Is it yours? Do you need to remove someone in your life? How does your fish tank look? Are you healthy staying in it?

Guardrails

I remember three years ago hearing a series called guardrails from a pastor named Andy Stanley. Audio books are one of my favorite things in the world. I don't always have time or want to make time to sit down and read. But I am constantly driving, so I now have a library on wheels with audio books. Audio books always give us an opportunity to receive some great insight in our lives versus filling our heads with music that most likely isn't giving us something good. And it doesn't take extra time in our lives. We all have the same amount of time in a day.

Most of us think of guardrails and think of the rails on the side of the road. What are they designed for? To keep us from harm and ending up in the ditch or other lanes of traffic. We would always rather hit a guardrail than end up in a ditch or oncoming traffic. I put guardrails in my life so I can stay on the road and not end up in the ditch. And I would always rather hit a guardrail I put in place than end up in a ditch. How about you? I love the analogy because guardrails have really helped me over the years in being intentional with who I am and who I am becoming.

I have put guardrails on my time, finances, and even my romance life, just to name a few. About three years ago, I got serious about purity in my relationships. My then girlfriend and I started dating, and even though neither of us were virgins, we decided we wanted God in every aspect of our lives, which included sex. I understand this isn't a decision for everyone, but it was a choice we made. It wasn't an easy one for me by any means. And by any means I mean it was extremely, extremely difficult. I don't think I'd ever went more than a couple months without sex since I was 20 years old. I slept around a lot and didn't care. I say all that because this was a big life change for me and a very hard next step. But I viewed woman the wrong way. I viewed what they could do for me and how they could validate me versus how I could take care of them. I viewed them as objects through my actions, and I knew that was unhealthy for me. I could never love someone or, especially a wife by doing that. So this was my next step.

My girlfriend, at the time, and I realized quickly we couldn't do this by shear willpower. We've come dangerously close so many times by breaking our own rule. We learned to set guardrails in our relationship.

I'm not saying anyone who is single should do this. I'm just being vulnerable with you with what we did. We said no more hanging out one on one past 9 p.m. and only in a group. At night, it was way too hard. We also said no sleepovers at all. If I ever had to stay over or went on a vacation, we slept in separate beds. I also made myself a guardrail of not hanging out with women after 9 p.m. unless they were family or in groups with other people. I couldn't resist. I know that might sound ludicrous to you, but I would rather bump into a guard rail than end up in a ditch. Sometimes we need to take extreme next steps so we get out of the ditch entirely.

I also have guardrails with my time and priorities. For example, while I am writing this book, I make sure it is the first thing I do every day when I wake up. After eating, praying, and letting the dog out, I sit down and write. I know I won't do it later after answering emails, having lunch with someone, going to the gym, or hanging out with people. If I wanted to finally finish this book, I needed to put my guardrails around my morning time and stick to it. I've turned down breakfasts with friends, texting people or being near my phone, social media in the mornings, to letting people bother me before noon. This was only until I completed my first rough draft. Sometimes guardrails are temporary, and sometimes permanent. What' I'm trying to say is we need to match our guardrails up with who we want to become. And the extent that we set up guardrails is related to how serious we are about taking our next steps or becoming who we were meant to be.

Unfortunately, many people don't set up guardrails until they end up in a ditch or until it's too late. We don't set up guardrails on dating, our time, our priorities, our families, our morals, or important friendships. A lot of times, we just get so busy with being busy that we just don't know who we are or why we are doing what we are doing anymore. I can't be the only one who has felt this way before. Putting up guardrails in my life has aligned my life in a direction to who I want Ito become and then the "doing" just naturally happens. Guardrails, in a way, are the narrow gates to a wide life.

It isn't a set of rules to follow. It's protecting who we are and being intentional with the life we have been given. For example, telling our 15-year-old daughter she needs to be home by 11 p.m. isn't being a rule-crazy father who doesn't want her to have any fun. It's putting guardrails in her life so she can't make decisions she will regret later. As a parent, it is done out of love, not rule following. It's protecting her because we know nothing good happens past 11 p.m. for our 15-year-old daughter. If we put guardrails up for children, why don't we do that for ourselves? We aren't any better once we really think about it. We are just as prone to mistakes as they are. We sometimes make worse mistakes than they do, and we can all act childish. Or is that just me? What are some guardrails you need to put in your life so you can become who you were meant to be? Someone amazing and impactful in this world. Guardrails are designed for us to keep our lives out of the ditch. They make us intentional and align our actions with who we are meant to be. If we aren't being intentional with our lives, then who will be?

Action steps/ Possible Next Steps/ Questions

Do you have a mentor?

If not, that's very common, but unless we want to live like everyone else we need to do what everyone else probably isn't doing. Who can mentor you? A teacher? An advisor? An uncle? Someone from your church? Someone's parent who you look up to?

A mentor is just someone you do life with and talk about things. You talk about the tough things and bounce next steps off of.

Do you need a bigger fishbowl?

How does you fish tank look?

Can you be healthy staying in your current environment?

Do you have anyone you need to remove from your life?

What guardrails do you need to put in your life so you can live in freedom versus worry?

Do you feel like you wait until you're in the ditch to finally think about guardrails in your life?

Chapter 5: Healthy Relationships

It Takes Two Healthy People to Have a Healthy Relationship.

Ever date someone and think you can change them? We say things like:

"They have some rough edges around them, but hey, don't we all?"

"Maybe they have more than the average person, but maybe I can change them."

We think, "I don't like that they do certain things, but if I spend a certain amount of time with them, they will change."

I know that's how some old girlfriends viewed me, and I know that's how I viewed some, as well. The problem with that solution or way of thinking is that we can't date people to change them. We date to love them and encourage them right where they are. People want to be loved right for who they are with no ulterior motives. Don't you? I've been in a relationship where I was the unhealthy one. In fact, I have always been the unhealthy one in the relationship when they were unhealthy. What I mean by that is I was trying to get from the other person what I didn't feel myself. I didn't feel love; therefore, I tried to get it from the other person. That exhausts a significant other, and it's unhealthy. I had old dad wounds I needed to get rid of before I could seriously be healthy in any relationship. Unfortunately, the girlfriends I had before sat through all that rage, rudeness, and unhealthiness. They had to sit through the performance poison that I put on myself. *If I do enough of (fill in the blank), I will become someone worth loving and I will become significant.* Remember? What we are looking for in life drives our behavior. Who we believe we are will determine our behavior (A dog barks. A cat meows). I've manipulated in relationships. I've had anger, and I've said a lot of mean things. I treated women as objects and said a lot of brutal words because that's what I learned growing up, and I thought it was normal. It shouldn't be, and it's not okay, I found out.

I learned growing up, if you are hurt, you hurt them back with words or, in some cases, violence. If an argument isn't going your way, you storm out. You don't stay and resolve it calmly without tearing each other down. You win at all costs, and it doesn't matter what is right. It's the principle, you know? I learned all these wrong things before my parents divorced. I was four or five at the time. I remember I wasn't allowed to play with kids in the neighborhood because I swore a lot. I had no idea I was a bad kid really. I thought it was normal. I had no idea how to treat women growing up. No one taught me, and what I learned from my childhood wasn't the greatest example. I learned when you argue, you raise your voice if you don't feel heard or understood. Maybe a slight shove would get it across that you aren't going to deal with a situation. I remember being blamed for the divorce by my father before he was forced to move out. I'm amazed I can remember all these moments in detail when I can't even remember to put the milk back in the fridge most mornings.

I think you can understand how I became an unhealthy person in relationships. I'm not here to blame. I'm here to tell you that if you grew up in a similar way, there is so much hope. And a lot of times, we are just doing the best we can with what we know. And sometimes, all we know is anger because of our past.

It took me a while to get over my anger. It took me a long time to see the unhealthiness in my heart and how I handled conflict the wrong way. I realized eventually how much pride was in my heart, and it was time to sit down and really start healing from it all. I was trying to heal from 20+ years and trying to reverse all my anger, bitterness, bad habits I learned. But I learned over time that I couldn't reverse it on my own. I needed mentors, and I needed great friends who had healthy relationships. I started hanging out with friends in healthy, loving, nurturing relationships. I started hanging out with great married guys from church. When I was single, that's all I did. I wanted to be around people I wanted to be like. And I wanted to have a healthy relationship in the future. I wanted to have a healthy marriage and be a great father. I wanted to reverse everything wrong and unhealthy that I learned. I needed a great support system to do that. Changing my environment, reading my Bible, and letting great Christian guys pour into me on a weekly basis really helped me take my next step in that direction of my life. It was a long journey of next steps, and man did I fail, like a lot. I thought I learned, and then I realized I still had hurt in my heart. But facing it head on and not ignoring it made all the difference. Talking about what I felt was wrong and why or how I did certain things with good mentors showed me what being a real man was all about. Maybe your next step is finding someone who has a really healthy relationship and spending time with them more often. Our environment shapes who we are.

I also want to say that I still can struggle with my past sometimes if I'm being honest. I can see pride choke up sometimes. I can see my old self show up from time to time. But it is not even close to where it used to be. I mean not even close. I am so thankful I have a wonderful, loving, caring woman in my life who gives me grace when I need it. She doesn't hold things against me, and I am so grateful to have Amber in my life. She doesn't bring up old arguments. She doesn't tell me what I'm doing wrong. She points me to Jesus, not my failures. She makes suggestions when she knows I'm not making the best decision and urges me to seek good counsel. She is thoughtful with her words and always wants what's best for people. She and I both come from similar backgrounds. Her father passed away when she was 15 years old. She's had a friend commit suicide. Her mother worked extremely hard like mine did to become an independent, single mom raising kids on her own. She's had brothers get arrested and thrown in jail. It's quite amazing how this sweet, loving, caring woman rose out of that situation. I'm thankful she did. She has such a heart for people with tough upbringings because of it. Amber would rather work in an under privileged school on the worst side of town than the nicest school district. I'm not sure how I got so lucky with a woman with an amazing heart and love for others. I'll stop writing before she changes her mind about marrying me.

What I want you learn from this section is that if you don't love someone right where they are or if they don't change, then it might not be in your best interest to date them. We can't change people. Women couldn't change me even though they tried. It takes two healthy people to have a healthy relationship. A healthy person can't make another person healthy in a relationship. If someone is doing something that is making your heart unhealthy or stopping you from becoming who you were meant to be, we can't make people change. I think you know what your next step is.

I want to encourage you right where you are to never settle. We don't have relationships to be loved but because we are already loved and make each other as Matthew Kelly says, "The best version of ourselves." How many people do we know that have been in a stagnant relationship because they don't have the energy to end it? They worry more about what-ifs versus what they should do. And then we see them getting married just because they are getting older or just because they've been together for so many years already. Is there real freedom there? Are there real freedom, joy, and purpose in settling because we are afraid of the unknown? I am 30 years old as I write this now, and I am so glad I ended my relationship at 28 years of age even though I invested almost two years into it. It was unhealthy for both of us. And she deserves someone great for her, as I do for me. Never settle. That is a next step we should never take. Never settle.

Leaders and Healthy Relationships Go First.

Leadership doesn't stop once we clock out for the day. It isn't a title we only have at work. The best leadership, in my opinion, is the leadership in s person's home and small circles. Some of the greatest CEO's have a great pulse on what's going on in their company but none on their wife or kids. They have no idea what's really going on in their kids' lives and are emotionally unavailable. They may be leading behind a desk or at their job but doing the exact opposite once they leave for the day. I know that was so true for me once upon a time. I'm not married and don't have any kids but there were times that as soon as I walked out of the office, my integrity and leadership mindset would stay at the office behind me.

We are all leaders, as I mentioned earlier in this book, and leaders always go first. I'm not talking about going first in the meeting room, coming up with a new idea, or being the first one in the building in the morning. I'm talking about going first in what really matters in the end. They go first when it comes to relationships, and that means any relationships, even the coworkers, their boss, the mailman, and the neighbor they might not like.

Healthy people go first when they see a conflict. They go first to stop the gossip when it starts. Next-Step Leaders go first in their relationships, despite who is wrong or at fault. Next-step leaders know who they are and aren't afraid of how they look like if they go first. They are comfortable with their identity.

There have been so many examples of arguments with my significant other. I swear in my head I know I'm right, and I can name specifically how I am right in those moments. But she doesn't see it. And even worse she's angry at me! How could she be when I am right?! Does this sound familiar to you?

Why We Go First

Man, if I had a dollar for every time I felt that way. Let me say this to you: You can be right, or you can be in a relationship. You usually can't have both. If we choose being right over the relationship, we have some next steps to take in the pride department. Or the relationship isn't that important to us. Does being right matter that much to us? "It's the principle!" we might say. Is the principle really that important? We can have pride, or we can be a leader. And leaders, real leaders, change the world by doing what most people don't do. We go first. We go first when no one else does. We take action. We don't ignore problems.

The weird thing is that we don't go first so we can BECOME leaders or just because it makes us feel good in the moment. We go first because we ARE leaders. Remember, identity determines behavior. We don't need to tell a fish to swim. It just does it. As leaders, we don't need to go first so we can become a leader. We just do it because that's what we are.

As leaders, we go first because it's who we are and because it sets us free in our own hearts. We can't lead when our heart isn't healthy, and a heart full of pride isn't a heathy heart. We can't give what we don't have, so maybe if we can't go first as a leader, we need to figure out where our pride is coming from, like a past hurt. Maybe we were taken advantage of before and don't want it to happen again? Join the club.

Maybe we were hurt and tried apologizing before, and it enabled a person to just keep hurting us. Yep, I've been there. I get that, and I know I've been there. But here is the thing - we don't apologize to change the person's behavior. We do it because we've been given grace when we didn't deserve it before. We give what we already have love and grace in our heart. So maybe your next step, if you can't go first, is to receive something today and to heal from a past hurt. That is a great next step, and that makes us one step ahead of others who aren't trying. There is more freedom for those who take their next steps.

What is Real Forgiveness?

I used to think forgiveness meant, "It's okay. It didn't matter anyways," which is why I didn't like apologizing. I felt apologizes meant I was wrong or that it didn't matter anyways, when it did. I felt apologizing was something I said when I felt like I was over the hurt or when I eventually felt better. I thought forgiveness had nothing to do with me but everything to do with the other person. It couldn't be further from the truth actually.

Did you ever get in trouble as a kid? Of course, you did. My nickname as a kid was "Dennis the menace". Don't know who that is? Google it. I was a kid always getting in trouble. When I beat up my brother or accidently hurt a kid, what was I always forced to say to the other kid? Sorry! It was a forced apology. Anything to get out of it and go back to playing. We think we are teaching kids how to apologize, but I feel like it taught me the wrong way of how apologizing really works. You see, when I said sorry to the kid or my brother, what was the natural response back from the other kid? "It's okay," or maybe "Thanks." Like we did them a favor? A small price to pay for pushing down a kid if you ask me. Maybe that's why I played so recklessly.

But this is where I missed it as a kid and where I think we all can miss it. Forgiveness doesn't mean it's okay. It doesn't mean the offense didn't matter. It doesn't mean it's water under the bridge or let's just move on. To me, forgiveness now means, "It did hurt. It wasn't right. It was wrong. But I release myself of the anger and resentment. It means, I give you grace because I needed it too in my life." Forgiveness doesn't just release the other person from bondage. In fact, it's not really about releasing the other person. It releases me from the hurt it gave me. It leads me into greater freedom in my life, and it will do the same in yours.

How many times in our lives do we say we forgive someone but still have resentfulness towards them? Is that really freedom for us? Is that the best we can do? I want to challenge that and say no. Far from it. A lot of times, forgiveness has more to do with us than the other person. It reveals more what's going on in our heart versus what actually happened.

Are there any areas of resentment in your heart towards someone? If so, why is that still there? Did their actions or words dig up something from your past? Maybe that's a next step for you take. I know I've had to get rid of a lot of resentment in my heart.

It took me years to forgive my dad and even my stepdad. But I want to tell you a little bit of my story.

I mentioned it briefly, but my stepdad left my family when I was 17 years old. Cold turkey. He said he was going to Chicago for the weekend to help his sister out with her restaurant and never came back. For 12 years, he wasn't a father to his two young daughters, who were two and eight when he left. He would call maybe once a year to see how they were doing. I never understood why that all happened. He was an alcoholic, and we do not make great choices when our hearts aren't healthy. I remember he came to visit when I was 22 or so. He wanted to make things right, and I was angry that he would show up out of nowhere. The way I saw it, he was an alcoholic since I was eight years old. He affected my childhood greatly, and now he has come back again? I didn't want any part of it. It didn't even last two days of him coming back that he was drinking again. Since I was older at the time, I asked firmly for him to leave, which he did a day later.

He was gone for another seven years and came back in the picture. This time, he was homeless and in real need. In all reality, you must be pretty desperate to reach out to your ex-wife for help when you haven't seen her in seven years. At this point in my life, I'd forgiven Tom a couple years back, when I was facing my father wound in my heart. I knew I truly forgave him and was free when I saw him at an Applebee's working as a waiter. I didn't feel any anger. I only felt empathy for him. I felt like I wanted to help. I remember buying him a Christmas present and gift card from the nearest grocery store. I wrote him a letter of how I had forgiven him and how I would love to help if he needed a ride or anything. The guy was homeless. We've all needed help. Yeah, some people say they "deserve what they get" or "had a million second chances," but aren't we all worth another try if we set healthy boundaries? I'm not inviting the guy to stay at my house, but I can lend a ride during winter, some food, and listening ear. We are all worth that. Aren't we all just worth another try? People used to think I wasn't.

My former step-dad and I went to the grocery store together a couple times. He needed a ride to and from the grocery store. Conversations arose, and I invited him to my church. We've been in contact since. I don't know where that is all going. No idea. But I want to say that if I can forgive an alcoholic stepfather of 12 years and a father who I couldn't legally meet until I was 14 and after more than his fair share of second chances, maybe you can take your next step in that department, as well? Jesus doesn't see messy people. He sees people in a mess. For me, I am not identified by what I've done wrong. I am identified by what Jesus has done right. I am; therefore, I do. And we can see people the same way. We can see people in a mess instead of identifying them as messy people. Which one is more freeing for us and for that person? I think we all know the answer.

Healthy Conflict

When most of us hear the word conflict we think it's a negative thing or can't be seen as good. It's not true. Confrontation or conflict can be positive. It can be a healthy. Most of us want to avoid conflict at all costs. We don't want to say anything when we know we should. Often we let good opportunities slip away because we just keep things in. And then they eventually blow up.

As I mentioned earlier, I never knew how to handle conflict well. I was taught through seeing that when we are hurt, we hurt others in return with our words. I was shown when we don't feel heard, we scream and yell. I was taught to leave when things got tough. It's amazing how much children can pick up things that they take with them the rest of our lives. We can teach our children all day what is right, but in the end, our actions are what our children and others learn. I've learned most everything the hard way. I knew what was right by others telling me, but sometimes, unfortunately, it didn't click until I learned enough times that my way wasn't working. Then I didn't want to do those actions anymore.

What You Heard and What They Said Might be Different.

I've learned this the past year with my significant other, Amber. Even though we are very similar, we couldn't be more opposite at the same time. And a lot of times, we hear something different than what we actually said to each other.

For example, Amber can say, "Dave, I don't feel like talking right now. Can we just talk about it later?" when I'm trying to tell her something or want to get something off my chest. In that moment, I can personally hear, "Dave, I don't care what you have to say. I'm more important and I don't respect you enough to stop what I'm doing to listen to you."

Did she say that? No. But that's what I heard. My past and how I'm wired triggered what I heard rather than what she actually said. I've learned to ask questions to clarify what I heard so I don't get in an argument over something that wasn't even meant a certain way. Sometimes, repeat back what you think they said, and see if you heard right. This has saved me a lot of trouble.

Blame

Often when I am angry or upset, I can quickly jump to conclusions or reasons why I didn't get my desired outcome. This can happen whether it be a sports game; an outcome at home, like food not being ready; or something that I expected to be done that just didn't come intro fruition. This happens a lot in relationships. We expect something done a certain way, and it doesn't happen. When this happened, I immediately jumped to blame and to why this wasn't my fault but the other person's. I didn't win because so and so didn't play well. The pizza should have been ordered already for the football party. The clothes should have been folded and put away like I was told. As you are probably aware, things often don't go as planned. The sooner I got that and stopped putting my identity in circumstances or results, I stopped being so angry all the time. What we put our identity in grows. This is why I can't put my faith in circumstances because they change so drastically. I wanted to get off the angry emotional rollercoaster. Do you? I've learned the wrong way probably thousands of times, that blaming someone never got me a good result. Changing what I put my identity was a huge part of it. I've realized keeping score in what someone has done for me and what I've done for them never gets me my desired result. And since when does keeping score in any type of relationship bring any of us more freedom?

Name Calling: We Never Want to Hurt Someone's Identity.

I can name countless times of my brother and I calling each other names growing up. Man, we would destroy each other with our words. We knew everything about each other, so we knew the words to get the other one fired up. We would tell each other our secrets and then use them against each other later. How brutal!

That didn't change when I had a girlfriend growing up or was close to women, in general. When I was hurt by them, I would pull out the things I knew would hurt them and would just fire at will. I would name call and say names I can't write in this book. I can feel pretty guilty thinking of what I called people.

The whole *sticks and stones can break my bones but words don't hurt me* BS is a lie. Words do hurt us, and they do shape us. They shape us tremendously. Words either build up or they tear down, and there is no in-between. There is some subtle truth in the sarcastic comments or jokes we make. There is some meaning behind all of our words. It's how we express ourselves. But name calling is so bad for relationships because it hurts the other person's identity. When we call someone something terrible, we are actually telling them who we think they are. For example, me calling someone a lair is telling them they don't live things truthfully, and that hurts them. Whether their actions reflect that name calling or not, it doesn't matter. Name calling will NEVER get us the result we want. We can say we think they are being untruthful with their words, but name calling doesn't have a place in a healthy relationship.

Let's focus on how they are making us feel versus name calling. For example, if I feel like I am being lied to, I will just come out and say that. "I feel like I am being lied to." You notice I am not blaming them or calling them a name. I am simply stating how I feel.

Instead of calling someone a provocative name out of being hurt or angered by what they said, I can simply state, "What was said right now really hurt me." No blame. No name calling, and it gets to the point. I want you to understand this next sentence. Read it twice actually. Anger is a subsidiary emotion of being hurt. Anger just means we were hurt by someone's action or words, but we mask our hurt with anger because we were conditioned a long time ago to fight back when we are hurt. Anger is a wall we put up to protect ourselves and man was I good at that for a long time. Unfortunately, I had to go through a lot of pain to understand that anger is a weapon that only friendly fires. It only hurts me in the end and puts the other person's walls up. No one wins.

Our Intelligence is Low When our Emotions are High.

So, when I feel that anger starting in my heart and stomach. I focus on why I feel that way and I just tell them how I feel versus blaming or name calling. If they decided to get angry or be rude after that I remove myself from that situation, why? Because when emotions are high, our intelligence is low. When we're angry or stressed, our body releases a chemical called Adrenaline. They called it the "Fight or flight" drug. So unfortunately, we either stay and fight or flight. Neither is always good, as you know. It also lowers our rational thinking because we are afraid we do things we usually wouldn't do under normal circumstances. So, when we try our best to calm the situation, don't blame, or name call, it's probably our best bet to cool off first before finishing the conversation. Let us both come to our senses. And if the other person wants to stop talking, it's probably best we do. Both parties need to be ready to have the conversation. We need two healthy people to have a healthy relationship.

Threats or Manipulation

When we are arguing with someone we know, we often times know their biggest fear or how to get what we want. I call them hot buttons. We know what triggers emotions or action from them. For example, I hated being threatened by a significant other that she would leave if something doesn't change or happen. My biggest fear was being abandoned. I'm sure that stemmed from my father wound, but I hated it when someone I loved wanted to end our relationship because something didn't happen. It would make me immediately want to fix what's going on. I was being manipulated, and my intelligence was too low to realize it most of the time. And when I did realize it, I didn't have the energy to do anything about it. I was too afraid of the unknown at the time. Fear often paralyzes or propels.

I would also manipulate, and, man, was I good at it. I remember years ago leaving flowers on a girlfriend's car when she wanted to break up. I remember using my words to get out of situations, and I remember lying to temporarily calm the storms. When I know what someone wanted to hear, I was good at shaping my words to have them hear what they wanted to hear. I learned this through sales and training thousands of sales reps during by my mid-twenties. I learned how to motivate and make people take action despite them being unsure about something. I would ask questions that I knew the answers to so it would make them think a certain way. I was good at playing chess with minds is what I'm saying. *If I do this, it will make them do this. Then in return they would do this, and that's when I say this.* Which in the end got me the result I wanted. It's pretty scary admitting it, but I was good at it; however, I learned that real love couldn't be manipulated. Real connection can't be manipulated or threatened. Real love casts out fear; therefore, I didn't need to manipulate anymore. The reason I tried to manipulate was because I thought I felt in control when I did it. But as with most things before, I learned the hard way. I never felt fulfilled in the end doing things the wrong way. In the end, it all catches up to us if we don't stop. Threats and manipulation have no place in a healthy relationship, a healthy work place, and a healthy leading environment. Manipulation is fake growth when leadership uses it.

So when others do these things to us like name calling, blame, or manipulation, remember before we get angry that most people are just doing what they learned in the past. They are doing the best with what they know, and a lot of times they think that's the best solution because it's what they grew up watching. Instead of seeing a messy person, we just need to see a great person in a mess, and we need to give them grace like we needed. And sometimes we need to just remove ourselves from the situation.

Never Remain in an Abusive Relationship

After saying everything you just read, I want to make a point. Grace is great, and seeing the best in people is awesome. But when we are in an abusive relationship, we need to get out of it immediately. No one deserves that, and that person can't heal or learn with you still in their life. Whether we are in a relationship or not, it is NEVER our job to change someone, regardless of whether we are married to them or just dating. Therefore, if we ever find ourselves in an abusive situation we need to give ourselves permission to leave it. We deserve better, and they can't get better with us there. We both lose if one stays. I hope you're not in that situation, but it is very common. There is no question that if you are in this predicament, that is your next step. Remove yourself from that relationship or environment. Again, you both lose if you stay. It stunts their growth because they are enabled when you stay, and it makes you unhealthy. No one wins. You both lose. Abusive relationships never end up good if we stay in them.

Questions:

What stuck out to you the most in this chapter?

What's your definition of forgiveness?

Where do you see the need for the biggest improvement?

Are YOU healthy?

What's your next step?

Chapter 6: Is being busy really worth it?

When we ask someone how they are or what's new, what's a common response? I usually get "Busy" or "Nothing". Am I the only one? Or I might receive the negative rant of the day if I'm lucky enough. Busy is by far the most popular answer I receive, and I just have to ask, is that a good thing? Is being busy a way we should always describe our life? Is it an accomplishment by today's standards?

For me, it's not about being busy. I care about being intentional. Am I being intentional with the time I am given? Am I being a good steward of my time left on earth? These are questions that I ask myself frequently. Some of us are just on cruise control in our life. But we can't take next steps while our lives are on cruise control. And if we aren't careful, a year or more goes by, and we wonder what we did with all that time we had. We were always busy but it meant nothing in the end. Have you ever felt like this? I know I have in the past.

Silence Brings Clarity

Have you ever been lost before while driving somewhere with your friends? Or maybe you've been on a road trip with your parents? Either way, I think we can all picture a moment in our lives when we were lost and the driver turned down the radio and yelled, "shut up!." Why does the driver demand silence when he or she needs to think? Because as Matthew Kelly once wrote, "Clarity emerges from silence." It's true. But do we like to be silent and still? If you are anything like me, the answer is no. I am usually go-go-go, and I'll stop and ask questions later. But the more time goes by the more I know I need to be intentional. I need to be quiet, so I can understand what's going on. I need to block out the white noise so I focus on what's really next for me. I often like to be quiet in the mornings and think about why and what am I doing that day. I often like to read my Bible. I like to pray and listen to see if God is speaking to me that day. I love how John Stickl puts it. "The real question isn't, is God speaking? It's, Are we listening?" I can't listen if I'm too busy moving. I can't listen if my ears are already listening to something else. I can't hear what my heart is saying to me if I'm too busy numbing it or staying busy.

Whenever I see college students on campus, I usually see most students wearing headphones of some kind. They are always listening to music. Very rarely do I see someone not staring at their phone or without headphones in their ears on campus. I wonder why this is. Why can't we walk in silence anymore without some kind of distraction? I mean, I love music just as much as the next person. Am I weird for driving in silence sometimes though? Is it really that difficult to sit in silence to think about what's going on with our lives in a healthy way versus just turning on a show or distracting ourselves constantly?

Is slowing down and being silent your next step?

The Piñata Game

There is an exercise I do sometimes when I speak to college students. I have the students destroy a piñata full of candy and money. I tell them ahead of time what's in it. I ask them who loved this game as a kid. I ask them who would dive in head first and try to get as much candy as they could get when they were little. Most students raise their hands. I'd ask which of them didn't care what people thought of them as a kid when we dive in for the candy. Most of them raise their hand again. I reiterated that we are going to relive that childhood dream again. There is some good candy in there. There are some $1 bills, some $5 bills, and even a few $20 bills. Does anyone need beer money for this weekend? I get a couple roars from the crowd from that one usually. And as someone destroys the piñata, the students would dive in relentless as I yell throw some elbows! I mean it's a blood bath. I'm just kidding about the blood bath, but it's exciting to see college students just dive on the floor recklessly. Maybe I should have them sign a waiver?

After everything is picked up and the laughing has subsided, I will ask them what they learned. The answer usually receive is the "Go for it when you want something." Good answer. I'll also usually hear "Don't care what people think and just go for it." Another good answer. And maybe you thought about why I did that exercise. I love doing it because it wakes them up after a while of me speaking to them. It gets the blood flowing. I do love the analogy though that follows after their answers. I'll just explain it to you as I would to them.

Do you remember going after the candy as a kid when the piñata broke open? The excitement that it created and the urgency. I mean, I would dive in there and try and fit as much candy as I could hold in my little hands. Do you remember who would get the most candy though? And if you do remember, what was the technique for the kid would get the most candy? If you are thinking what I'm thinking of, the kid who always got the most candy was the kid that took both arms out like he or she was about to hug a tree and just pulled all the candy in towards their body. The child would get most of the candy, and I remember thinking *Wow, that is so smart! I'm going to do that from now on!* But you know what happened to that kid usually? What did he or she have to do afterwards when some kids didn't get any candy? He would need to give some of that candy away because he monopolized the system, and other kids didn't get some candy. The kid was usually resentful he had to give some away but he usually did right? We think, *well that kid will learn someday that is the right thing to do. He's just too immature to know that now.* But do we ever really learn? Or does it get worse actually? I think it often gets worst as we grow up.

Success can Actually Hurt Us from Taking our Next Steps

I don't know about you, but I don't want to lose what I have gained in life. Like the kid who gained the most candy, I would think, *well, that's life!* The entrepreneur side of me says the kid should keep it since he or she was smart enough to think ahead of time what to do. I would also think this shows the kids what life is like if we don't go after what we want. All these things would roll through my mind. Maybe I shouldn't admit this? But in all seriousness, it's a great opportunity to show kids that when we are given so much, we can give so much. That we aren't here to gain everything because we already have everything we need. For me I have everything in Jesus; therefore, everything else is gravy. More possessions don't equal more happiness. I've tried that route.

Anyways, sometimes I can have a hard time parting with what's in my mind, something I worked hard for. And sometimes, however, that is what stops us from taking our next steps and becoming who we were meant to be. After we gain more in life, we can think this is good enough. "I'm happy here." And we might be, at least for now. But just like anything else, things grow stale after a while. We lose that new car smell, that new kitchen feel, new vacations turn into just vacations. We miss opportunities to release love, freedom, and grace and to help others along the way. What I'm saying is we don't give our extra candy away even though we couldn't eat it all any ways. Or if we do, we get a tummy ache. If we aren't intentional we may never grow out of that childlike mindset. The *more is better* mentality. And without even realizing it, we subconsciously are growing walls in our heart and slowly start having an apathetic heart because we think it will never be enough. We stop taking next steps. We think, *why should we?* And you might be fine with that and if you are than so am I. But if I may be blunt, if you keep going down that road, you will miss out on freedom and purpose that you were meant to experience. In the end, everything we own, all our possessions, our vacations, our titles, our preferences, they don't matter as much as we think they do. Who we are becoming is way more important than what we are doing.

Life Isn't about How Comfortable We Can Be

When we are too busy holding on to what we have, we can't have open hands to receive our next step. Every next step we take brings us into greater freedom and purpose and shows us more of who we're meant to be. It gets rid of the

"I need to have this" mentality, and it takes our identity off possessions and comfort. Why do most of us think life is about being as comfortable as possible? Some of us think life's about how many Netflix shows we can cram in this week or how little work we can get away with, and the most exciting thing we can muster up is when our next vacation is. Why is that? Because sometimes, we put our identity in comfort, but that's not a life of freedom. That's a life of trying to self-medicate the mundane part of our lives like work, school, lack of energy, and purpose. Maybe instead of seeking our next show binge, we should be seeking our next step.

The worst part is that, when we do this, we enable and create an environment in which others feel comfortable doing the same. Isn't life more than a countdown to our next vacation? I mean this as life giving as possible when I ask this. When you go on vacation or are thinking about going on a vacation, are you more excited about discovering parts of the world, or are you just trying to escape your life? Are we more excited about being with people we love, or you just can't wait to drink? I've been on the end of the "I can't wait to go to the pool bar so I can just drink as many drinks as I can or want." I've been there, and I am not judging. I just want to ask, "Is that what our lives have come to?" Looking forward to just medicating ourselves? Because that's what it is. I mean, I'm all about having a good craft beer, but sometimes I have to ask myself *why am I having a drink?* Is it to be social so I can fit it in? Is it because I had a rough day? I never thought about this until I had to give up drinking for 12 weeks through a program called "Fight Club" at church. Yeah, you read that right. Accept we weren't fighting each other. The program was based on Nehemiah 4:14. We were fighting for our families, and, in my case, my immediate family, and future family. One of the rules we had was no alcohol for three months. Now, I had no idea how hard that was because I'm not a big drinker. I mean, I would drink a lot when I was in college, but once I started maturing as an adult, I drank maybe once or twice a week and just a beer per sitting. During that 12-week challenge of no alcohol, I started realizing how much I wanted a beer when others did. I realized very quickly how much of a social thing it was. I mean even my friends would egg me on "come on have a beer. Who cares about the rule?" I was surprised by the social pressure, and I was surprised by how much I wanted one. I didn't think I would care, but I was wrong. I realized I cared a lot more what people thought about me. And I realized I had a next step to take in that area of my life. I now question why I want a drink when I am out with friends and family, and I've thought about giving up drinking all together. I just really like trying craft beers from around the world. I don't need a whole beer. I just want to taste it because I love discovering new things. Maybe I have a next step to take?

Why Do We Go on Vacations?

I've become more intentional with my vacations. Am I going so I can post a picture on social media? Am I going just because I can? I don't have a life I want to escape from, but I used to when I worked sixty to eighty hours a week. I also want to mention that I am all about relaxing. In fact, I rented a cabin this weekend in the Adirondack Mountains to relax with my girlfriend and dog. She has a full-time job and is a full-time college student. She rarely has two days off in a row at this season of her life, so I thought I'd surprise her for a couple days of solitude in the mountains. Breathing in fresh air, going for a hike, taking in the great view on Lake Champlain, and just being silent. This isn't about escaping life. This is about resting, refocusing, and spending time with the girl I love. It's a great way for her to recharge. She loves teaching in the inner city of Buffalo. I mean, she loves it, and she can't wait to teach English as a second language to refugees as they literally escape terrible lives from another country. Maybe being intentional with why you vacation could be a next step? Maybe instead of seeking comfort all the time, we just seek our next steps?

Holding on to What We Have Gained Doesn't Let Us Receive What's Next.

To wrap everything together from the piñata game analogy, we can be too busy holding on to what we have gained. We can hold onto our preferences, way of life, job titles, a certain way we look, or a dating relationship that isn't right for us long-term. I like keeping things, as well, but like a kid, if we are holding on too tightly onto what we have been given or gained, it will eventually stop us from receiving more. You see, when we're younger or are young we will risk everything, despite what people think, to get something more often. As kids we will do anything to sneak cookies from the cookie jar or cupboard. We will dive on the ground for candy that cost barely anything. As young adults, we will try asking that girl, despite maybe feeling like an idiot if she turns us down. We will do anything to move up in that job. We will go the extra mile, and a lot of times, we don't care what people think because we are too busy trying to get ahead. In other words, we are totally okay with risking some things to gain more because we don't have much to lose at that point.

But the problem with success is that sometimes we gain more, and then our hands are full. We then shy away from any risk that isn't really calculated. Why?!? Why do we stop risking it? Because we are afraid to lose what we have gained. And success or what we have can stop us from our potential.

We no longer take next steps because we think to ourselves, *well I can't!* We think it's too risky. I'm not talking about just in business, but also in our lives, in general. We stop trying to gain new friendships because we hold onto friendships that we know aren't lining up with who we want to be. We hold onto that job because it's comfortable, and we are content. But we know every day we do that job, we just become more apathetic because it doesn't engage our heart or purpose anymore. We don't have the energy to find something different, or we think there is no hope. Another way this might look is that, when we get too busy with our lives, we stop dating our spouses. We think dating stops at marriage, and we stop putting our relationship first. Jobs, business, kids, and sports all become a higher priority than ourselves, and we eventually run out of energy to care anymore about each other. Apathy starts to set in.

What I'm trying to say is that we don't spread our arms out anymore because, if we do, we fear we might lose what we have already gained. And that's what stops us from becoming who we were meant to be and from living a life of freedom. I don't know what you're going through right now, but I do know we all have a next step to take. When we aren't taking next steps and not being intentional with our lives, we are also missing the opportunity as leaders to show others (and your family and friends) that, despite what success we have, we are never done taking next steps. We create an environment of empowerment, freedom, and purpose. Not stagnation, entitlement, and a "fend for ourselves" mentality. Success can actually hurt us from becoming who we were meant to be because we can stop taking next steps when we are more focused on what we have done than what next step we should take. We think we have already arrived. And someone who already thinks they have arrived can't go any further. They arrived, remember?

I don't want to be the grown up with his hands around the candy, not wanting to give it up. Instead of candy, we are holding onto our preferences, our title at our job that we worked so hard for, our house, cars, income, or that relationship.

We can't receive any more if our hands are already full. Sometimes, we need to let go of something that is dragging our heart down so we can become free. Sometimes, our next step isn't to do something, but to let go of something. Most of the time, our next step isn't adding anything, but subtracting dead weight in our hearts and time. What's your next step?

We Don't Have a Doing Problem; We Have a Receiving Problem.

When was the last time most of us woke up and said, "I have nothing to do today"? It's pretty rare. We have our jobs, our kids, our to-do lists, our doctor appointments, our events, our sporting events, or kids' events. As students, we have homework, essays, student activities, social events, relationships, planning, midterms, finals, spring break to plan, and jobs or internships to work or apply for. Things can get overwhelming pretty quickly. And then on top of it, people tell us what we need to do. We need to do this so we can get ahead or so we can become someone. We need to do this because it's the right thing to do. I don't know about you but I can get pretty sick of being preached at by so many people. So many people claim to know what to do with our lives and how to run them perfectly. That was part of my fear of writing this book. I don't want to come across as a know-it-all because I don't know everything. Far from it. I just want help people take next steps, tell my story, and teach what I've learned to help others live a life of empowerment and freedom.

When people usually think of a next step, they think of them doing something or adding something onto their to-do list. Not always, but usually. I think often our next step is to take something off our to-do list. Sometimes, it's to give less time to things that don't matter, bring us down, or don't bring us freedom in our lives.

Often, I will bring a big object for a student to hold when I am speaking. I call him or her up and ask them to hold a lot of things, like 20 stuffed animals. After the student has been given so much and clearly can't hold not even one more thing, I then try to hand her one more thing, and I say, "This is your next step right here. I want to give it to you. It's going to bring you so much more freedom in your life. It will walk you into your next purpose. It's a hard next step, but it's worth it! So just grab it and just receive it." I then try to hand her the stuffed animal or object, but she just can't. She has no capacity to hold it. Her hands are too full. She ends up dropping everything to try and grab the next-step stuffed animal. I think that is too often such a great picture of our lives. We are just overwhelmed with "stuff". It may be important stuff in our minds and maybe actually important, but we are so busy and overwhelmed. You might be reading this book and say, "Well, I don't have time to take next steps." Well you are right; you don't. More on that in the next paragraph. But we can't receive our next step or take our next step if our lives are already full. If we don't have the mental or physical capacity to do it, we won't take our next step. In today's world most of us don't have a doing problem. We have a receiving problem. Our to-do lists are never done, and we barely have enough energy to keep up with it. And it never feels complete. It just grows longer, and most of the time, we don't even want to do most of the things on the list. Listen, I want everything for you and nothing from you in this book. What is your heart telling you to do with some of the "stuff" on your to-do list? Is everything that important? Do we have to do everything at once? Are we more focused on what we are doing than who we are becoming? Are we trying to become significant rather than knowing we already are significant? Maybe your next step is to receive more instead of do more.

Every Time We Say Yes to Something, We are Saying No to Something Else.

I'll speak for myself here. I catch myself being busy a lot of times for the sake of being busy. I don't want to just sit around, and if I'm not intentional, I will catch myself putting my identity in being busy. Being busy might mean to me that I'm being productive because I learned from the world growing up being productive and being busy are important. I learned from self-help books not to be lazy, go after what you want, and don't make excuses. I always wanted to do something so I could earn the praises of others and so I could be someone worth mentioning or looking up to. I eventually found that to be exhausting.

When we are saying *yes* to something during our day, we are saying *no* to something else. The parent that works too much might be saying no to time with his or her kids. The college student that might spend too much time video gaming is missing out on a great campus experience, meeting new people, trying new things, and learning more about what is out there in the world. The young adult that is spending time with a friend or in a relationship that doesn't align with who he or she wants to be is saying no to a possible relationship that does align with their desired identity. He or she is saying no to more freedom in life and who he or she wants to be. I know I've been there.

Yesterday I had to say no to the gym to say yes to taking my dog to the park. My dog hasn't had much exercise the past few days, and the little guy deserved some time to get out of the house. Sometimes a *yes* means releasing freedom more in other people's lives than ours. Every situation is different. We can't say yes to everything, and we shouldn't always say no to everything. When we are going through our calendars and our to-do list, it helps to ask ourselves which ones align with who we are. Does that activity take us to where we really want to go? It's not always about us, but sometimes it is, as well. If we aren't healthy, we can't live a healthy life, and we can't give what we don't have. We can't help others if we aren't helping ourselves first. We hear it often- "It's not about you." Well maybe it is.

Questions:

Often, we are so busy with our lives that we can stop and reflect. When was the last time you sat and reflected on yourself?

Do you have more of a doing problem (Not enough action) or more of a receiving problem? (Can't sit still)?

Where can you get rid of apathy in your life?

A lot of times I can put my identity or my worth in what I'm doing verses what Jesus has already done for me. What about you?

Do you feel like you're more excited about vacationing or what's going on in your life personally?

What do you need to let go of so you can receive more freedom/joy in your life?

Chapter 7: There is ALWAYS a Next Step to Take

"There will be times of testing, times of proving, every thought will tell you "It's not going to happen". But don't believe those lies. Keep being Faithful, right where you are. "

I have no idea where I received that quote. But that quote is written on my white board in my home office. I see it often, and it's a great reminder when I'm facing challenges. Often, we can doubt our next step. It can be scary sometimes. Often, our next step is the hardest one to take. That's why most of us don't take it unless we have to. I don't want this to come across as hubris or egotistical, but I was never too afraid to my next steps. Sure, there were some really hard next steps. But I knew everything would be okay, and I always loved underdog stories. I wouldn't mind being one, and often, taking next steps makes us an underdog story. I think that's what God loves actually. He will stack the deck against himself just to prove it was Him. If we always take calculated risks, then how can we experience miracles in our lives? Maybe the lack of miracles in our lives is because we try to control everything too often?

Run the Play

I remember when Pastor John Stickl used this analogy in one of his sermons. I loved it, and I use it in a lot of my speeches. He uses the analogy from a football game. A coach calls in a play for the offense to run, and the offense lines up to run the play. They know it; they learned it, and they have practiced It over and over again. Everything they have gone through in the game has lead them up to this point. They just need to run the play, and now is the time to do so. The center goes to hike the ball, but instead of doing that, the entire offense just stands up and gives each other a high five! They say great job! We knew the play! That would have been awesome if we actually ran it right?!? How weird would that be if they did that and never ran the play? The game wouldn't go on if everything they knew they were supposed to do just didn't happen. Well, how often do we do this in our lives? We know our next step, but we don't do it. We know in our hearts what our next step or play is, but we just don't run it. We miss out on the purpose and freedom that could have been received by taking our next step.

I do remember the hardest play I had to run in recent years. It was a couple years ago actually when I just started running and owning a franchise for a publishing company. I didn't start the company. I just owned the franchise in Buffalo for it. It's not as cool as it sounds, but here I was starting it. I didn't get paid until I made a certain amount of sales and made it through the ramp up period. Well, I did that but because It took a bunch a of months, I was behind on my bills. I risked everything to start this business, and I'm finally getting paid for it. But there was a problem. I owed my mother some money still that she lent me when I was in ramp up. She needed the money to send one of my sisters to her first semester to college. I got paid once a month from the publishing company. That was the way it was set up. I budgeted my money like I usually did and had everything planned out for that month's paycheck. After paying my mother back, my bills, mortgage etc., I would barely, and I mean barely, have enough money for gas and food for the month. It was perfect how the money ran out perfectly so everyone got what they needed. Accept there was one problem. I forgot to factor in my tithe for the church I attend. I give 10% of my earnings before taxes to God every month. I forgot to factor it in that month unfortunately. I realized immediately, if I tithed, I wouldn't be able to pay all my bills for the month, let alone eat and have gas to do my appointments for work. I had a decision to make, and it was a big one. At least it was a big one for me.

Everything ran through my head. "Well my church doesn't need my money. They don't even know I tithe basically. I do it online, and they've never asked me. I just do it on my own. I mean I know they wouldn't care because it isn't about the money; it's about freeing my heart from money." I mean, I'm literally thinking all this in my head trying to justify why I don't need to tithe this month. But I knew in my heart that was a great next step for me. I immediately thought and said to myself out loud, "If God is who he said he is, did what He said He did, and is going to do what He said He is going to do, then I don't have to worry." I knew in my heart this was a next step in my faith and following Jesus. I donated the money before I could change my mind. And I had no idea, and I mean no idea how I was going to eat that month, pay some of my bills etc. I cried as I shut my laptop. That's the truth. I cried because I was so happy yet scared at the same time. I was happy I had the faith to do that, and I knew that was my next step. But now, what the heck am I going to do this month? I'm not going to reborrow money. That's not an option. I guess rice and beans is on the menu, and I will need to walk to my appointments or something. In all honesty, I had no idea what I was going to do, but this was a next step for me.

It wasn't four days later the company I worked for called me. They called me to tell me that they made a mistake with an order about three months earlier. I had no idea. They said they were sorry and they would be sending me a bonus to my bank account the next day. The bonus was five times more than what I tithed four days earlier. It was a big bonus. I couldn't believe it. I called all the other franchise owners across the country and asked if that mistake ever happened to them. It hadn't they said and the company has been around for 11 years at that point. What are the odds and what are the odds of it happening to me? That week? After I decided I was going to let go something so I can receive something better, having no idea what was going to happen? I hope this raises your faith like it did for me.

Sometimes, we are too busy holding onto what we have, so we miss out on a blessing that God wants to give us. I'm not saying that mistake wouldn't have happened with the order if I didn't tithe. What I'm saying is that I would have missed out on my next step to see how good God is if I didn't. I would have missed out if I didn't run the play.

How much of us are missing out on what God has for us because we are just too afraid to take our next step? We are afraid to run the play. I'm not saying you are going to get what you are asking for if you take your next step. What I'm saying is that we take next steps, not to receive a favor but because we are already favored. We take next steps to see more of who we are, who we're created to be and walking in freedom and purpose. For me, personally, it is about partnering and walking with God every day to release His love and grace in the world. It's about engaging my heart by aligning mine with His. It was never about building my kingdom. It was about building His. It was never about what I was doing. It's about who I am becoming in the journey and learning more of who God is. And that is someone good.

God Uses Imperfect People to Do the Impossible.

I have this on my white board as well in my house. It wouldn't take you too long to dig to find some dirt on me. In fact, you probably wouldn't even have to dig. I fail all the time. I don't always do things that align with who I am or want to be. I fail and try to control things sometimes when I feel the need to. I can try to plan so far ahead that I'm seeking more of my wisdom versus what God has planned for me. I can try to build my own platform sometimes instead of always giving God the platform. I can say some really dumb things sometimes. I can be ignorant and just closed-minded often.

But I am in good company. And there is so much freedom for me in admitting that I don't measure up all the time. God has and always will use imperfect people to do the impossible. He used Moses, who was a murderer and had a speech problem, to free the slaves out of Egypt. He used prostitutes, tax collectors, and a woman who was divorced five times. He used David, who was the least of his five brothers, to slay Goliath. David then became King and slept with another man's wife and had her husband killed. He used him too. He used Paul, who killed Christians for a living, and he became one of the greatest followers of Jesus ever and practically wrote most of the New Testament. I would say I am in good company if I fall very short. What I want to say is join the club if you don't feel qualified. I'm not qualified, but I am a beloved son because of Jesus and what He did. There is no scoreboard. There is no "Well, I'm doing more good than bad, and I'm a good person." It was never about that. That's behavior modification, and that's not what Jesus died for. You notice if you read the New Testament, Jesus never really hung out with the "religious people". He wanted nothing to do with them. He came for the lost, the broken, and the ones who couldn't help themselves. We don't need a doctor if we are sick. We don't need Jesus if we are too busy trying to qualify ourselves and bring joy into our own lives ourselves. I've tried that. I've made six figure incomes since I was 23 years old. I've vacationed in a lot of places, and I used to think *well I am a pretty good person because I help people and I do a lot of things for people.* I was still very imperfect and still very much am. Man, that feels good to say that. God used imperfect people to do the impossible. And He can use you. God doesn't need anything from us. He just wants everything for us. I don't need to do anything. I want to take next steps because His grace empowers me every day. What we believe about ourselves comes out in our actions. If we are empowered, we just naturally do things by what empowers us. I am empowered to write this book and share my story.

Be Vulnerable. The World Needs It.

That is the last thing written on my white board. Often when I was writing this book, I was thinking, "this is too much" and "that's too much information. Too vulnerable. What are people going to think?" Man, it was hard to write this book sometimes and scary for me to release this. Some people who have been with me my whole life had no idea all this stuff existed within me. Maybe they did; I don't know. Maybe I should ask them. But this is my next step. And sometimes we have no idea how this next step is going to go. Some people might think I'm weird for writing all this. I'm okay with that. I just know that I can't move forward without being fully me. This book is me. This is what I would give up my life for. The words and thoughts in this book. This is what drives me every day. This is what makes life so authentic for me. I'm willing to be vulnerable. I'm willing to go out on a limb, and I want others to do so with a life full love and their authentic self moving forward. There is never going to be another you in the world. Embrace that.

I seriously pray this encourages you to keep taking next steps. We never graduate from taking next steps. There is no riding off into the sunset. There is no "I have arrived" speech. It's "I took this next step. And this showed me this. And then I took this next step and then this was revealed. I then took my next step after that and more freedom came my way." Every next step shows us who we are and what we were created to do and empowers us to live a life of freedom and purpose. What's your next step?

A Kitchen Table Conversation

I want to encourage you where you are. First of all, you didn't have to read this book. Not all of it anyways, but you did. We live in a busy world, and there are millions of books to read. You chose to read mine. I'm grateful for that, and I'm grateful for you. You have gifts that I don't have. Please don't waste them. You have a circle of influence and people that I will never meet. You have people in your life that I can't impact and just can't reach. You have a destiny that I could never fulfill. You have a purpose in your life that I can't figure out for you. But you have a big purpose in your life. And despite anything you've done wrong, you can walk into freedom today, and God wants to use you. You are not your past. You are His future. I believe you are going to take next steps today, not because I need you or because you have to, but because you are just becoming who you already are: someone amazing. You are wired in a unique way with a unique and significant plan for your life. While others are focused on what they did wrong or what is going wrong, you are focused on what's next for you. You are enough right where you stand. You have what it takes. You are already loved and are worthy of love despite anything you've done. You have nothing to prove to anyone. You are an amazing person that is ready to change the world one next step at a time. I am so proud of you today just for being here and willing to read and receive all this even though we may have never met. I want nothing from you today. I just want everything for you. I want you to feel empowered today and just take a next step on your journey. And then take another step. I believe breakthrough is going to happen today for some of you here. I believe that things that are holding you back will no longer do that. We are all a work in progress. Keep taking your next step to become who you were already meant to be.